Minnesota Twins 2019

A Baseball Companion

Edited by Patrick Dubuque, Aaron Gleeman and Bret Sayre

Baseball Prospectus

Craig Brown and Dave Pease, Consultant Editors
Rob McQuown and Harry Pavlidis, Statistics Editors

Copyright © 2019 by DIY Baseball, LLC.
All rights reserved

This book or any part thereof may not be reproduced or transmitted in any form or by any means, electronic or mechanical, including photocopying, recording, or by any information storage and retrieval system, without permission in writing from the publisher.

Limit of Liability/Disclaimer of Warranty: While the publisher and the author have used their best efforts in preparing this book, they make no representations or warranties with respect to the accuracy or completeness of the contents of this book and specifically disclaim any implied warranties of merchantability or fitness for a particular purpose. No warranty may be created or extended by sales representatives or written sales materials. The advice and strategies contained herein may not be suitable for your situation. You should consult with a professional where appropriate. Neither the publisher nor the author shall be liable for any loss of profit or any other commercial damages, including but not limited to special, incidental, consequential, or other damages.

Library of Congress Cataloging-in-Publication Data:
paperback
ISBN-13: 978-1-949332-16-2

Project Credits
Cover Design: Kathleen Dyson
Interior Design and Production: Jeff Pease, Dave Pease
Layout: Jeff Pease, Dave Pease

Baseball icon courtesy of Uberux, from https://www.shareicon.net/author/uberux

Ballpark diagram courtesy of Lou Spirito/THIRTY81 Project, https://thirty81project.com/

Manufactured in the United States of America
10 9 8 7 6 5 4 3 2 1

Table of Contents

Foreword v
    Rob Mains

Statistical Introduction vii

Part 1: Team Analysis

Table for Two: Previewing the 2019 Minnesota Twins 3
    Mike Bates and Aaron Gleeman

Performance Graphs 7

2018 Team Performance 8

2019 Team Projections 9

Team Personnel 10

Target Field Stats 11

Twins Team Analysis 13

Part 2: Player Analysis

Twins Player Analysis 18

Twins Prospects 105

Part 3: Featured Articles

The Hole in The Shift is Fixing Itself 119
    Russell Carleton

The State of the Quality Start 123
    Rob Mains

Heads-Up Hacking—The First Pitch 129
    Matthew Trueblood

A Hymn for the Index Stat 135
    Patrick Dubuque

Index of Names 139

Foreword

Rob Mains

Welcome to this companion of the 2019 Minnesota Twins. We at Baseball Prospectus are excited to provide this analysis of the Twins.

Our website, Baseball Prospectus, is a leader in delivering high-quality commentary and data to baseball fans everywhere. To some, those words—commentary and data—appear mutually exclusive. There are people out there who believe that traditional analysis and advanced analytics must run on different paths. But the simplistic narrative of stats vs. traditionalists just isn't true. Every team's analytics department interacts with scouting, development, and major league operations with a common goal: Delivering a championship. New technologies, like radar tracking of pitch speeds and movement, enable talent evaluators to focus on qualitative aspects of pitching like mechanics and pitch sequencing. In-game strategies like infield shifts, based on batters' hit tendencies, help turn balls in play into outs. Hitters use information to adjust their swings to maximize run production.

All these numbers can seem, at best, intimidating, and at worst, counterproductive to the casual fan. Even as technology and analysis have embedded themselves deeply into the way teams run, it can often feel like statistics create a displacement between the viewer and the sport, breaking them out of the action. And yet every fan incorporates the numbers to some degree; stats like batting average and earned run average, so fundamental to how we talk about performance, are actually complicated formulas. They don't bother people because those formulas have become second nature, as easy to translate as the action on the field.

Along the way, new statistics have entered baseball's lexicon. You'll see some of them, like on-base percentage (which measures a batter's ability to get on base via walk, hit batter, or hit), OPS (on-base plus slugging), and average exit velocity (the speed of balls off a hitter's bat) on broadcasts. Others, like DRC+, might well be new to you. Some of them have been well-defined to the public, others haven't. That lack of context has created ambiguity. Fans know that a ball hit 100 mph is scorched, but does that mean extra bases? (Not if it's hit on the ground or high in the air it doesn't.)

For those who are amenable to them, the new statistics can increase the enjoyment and understanding of the game. They can help fans identify when a pitcher is tiring, when a stolen base or a bunt attempt makes sense (and, more often, when it doesn't), or how a team's lineup might be constructed. Websites like Baseball Prospectus add to that understanding by weaving metrics into the narrative of the game. That's the goal of this publication: to take some of the newer, more complicated statistics and make them as intuitive as the ones on the back of old baseball cards.

But you don't need to love analytics to love baseball. The fans at BP who worked together to write this guide are captivated first and foremost by the game itself. We're drawn to Aaron Judge's power, Francisco Lindor's glove, Billy Hamilton's speed and Patrick Corbin's slider and don't need numbers to tell us why they're so mesmerizing. The underlying statistics provide depth to the game that we all love.

We hope you'll find that this guide helps you better understand the Twins. Our analysts have studied the team's major league personnel and its minor league affiliates to identify their strengths and weaknesses, both the obvious ones and those that only a careful dissection of players' performances—yes, including the data—can reveal. You don't need us to tell you who was good and who wasn't in 2018, but our models and writers can help you project how each player is going to perform this year and beyond, and appreciate the greatness of each new game as it unfolds. As in the sport itself, the human and analytic components combine to generate a deeper overall understanding.

Think back to the first time you saw a baseball game on a high-definition TV. You'd grown familiar with how the game looked and felt on a picture tube. But new TV allowed you to see details that you'd never seen before. That's how advanced statistics work. The game itself is why you're here and why you're buying this. (And, for that matter, why we wrote it.) The statistical measures provide the sharper focus, the detail, the depth of knowledge that you didn't have before, generating an overall superior picture. Enjoy the view.

—*Rob Mains is an author of Baseball Prospectus.*

Statistical Introduction

Sports are, fundamentally, a blend of athletic endeavor and storytelling. Baseball, like any other sport, tells its stories in so many ways: in the arc of a game from the stands or a season from the box scores, in photos, or even in numbers. At Baseball Prospectus, we understand that statistics don't replace observation or any of baseball's stories, but complement everything else that makes the game so much fun.

What stats help us with is with patterns and precision, variance and value. This book can help you learn things you may not see from watching a game or hundred, whether it's the path of a career over time or the breadth of the entire MLB. We'd also never ask you to choose between our numbers and the experience of viewing a game from the cheap seats or the comfort of your home; our publication combines running the numbers with observations and wisdom from some of the brightest minds we can find. But if you *do* want to learn more about the numbers beyond what's on the backs of player jerseys, let us help explain.

Offense

At the end of this past year, we've revised our methodology for determining batting value. Long-time readers of Baseball Prospectus will notice that we've retired True Average in favor of a new metric: Deserved Runs Created Plus (DRC+). Developed by Jonathan Judge and our stats team, this statistic measures everything a player does at the plate–reaching base, hitting for power, making outs, and moving runners over–and puts it on a scale where 100 equals league-average performance. A DRC+ of 150 is terrific, a DRC+ of 100 is average, and a DRC+ of 75 means you better be an excellent defender.

DRC+ also does a better job than any of our previous metrics in taking contextual factors into account. The model adjusts for how the park affects performance, but also for things like the talent of the opposing pitcher, value of different types of batted-ball events, league, temperature, and other factors. It's able to describe a player's expected offensive contribution than any other statistic we've found over the years, and also does a better job of predicting future performance as well.

The other aspect of run-scoring is baserunning, which we quantify using Baserunning Runs. BRR not only records the value of stolen bases (or getting caught in the act), but also accounts for a runner's ability to go first to third on a single or advance on a fly ball.

Defense

Where offensive value is *relatively* easy to identify and understand, defensive value is ... not. Over the past dozen years, the sabermetric community has focused mostly on stats based on zone data: a real-live human person records the type of batted ball and estimated landing location, and models are created that give expected outs. From there, you can compare fielders' actual outs to those expected ones. Simple, right?

Unfortunately, zone data has two major issues. First, zone data is recorded by commercial data providers who keep the raw data private unless you pay for it. (All the statistics we build in this book and on our website use public data as inputs.) That hurts our ability to test assumptions or duplicate results. Second, over the years it has become apparent that there's quite a bit of "noise" in zone-based fielding analysis. Sometimes the conclusions drawn from zone data don't hold up to scrutiny, and sometimes the different data provided by different providers don't look anything alike, giving wildly different results. Sometimes the hard-working professional stringers or scorers might unknowingly inflict unconscious bias into the mix: for example good fielders will often be credited with more expected outs despite the data, and ballparks with high press boxes tend to score more line drives than ones with a lower press box.

Enter our Fielding Runs Above Average (FRAA). For most positions, FRAA is built from play-by-play data, which allows us to avoid the subjectivity found in many other fielding metrics. The idea is this: count how many fielding plays are made by a given player and compare that to expected plays for an average fielder at their position (based on pitcher ground-ball tendencies and batter handedness). Then we adjust for park and base-out situations.

When it comes to catchers, our methodology is a little different thanks to the laundry list of responsibilities they're tasked with beyond just, well, catching and throwing the ball. By now you've probably heard about "framing" or the art of making umpires more likely to call balls outside the strike zone for strikes. To put this into one tidy number, we incorporate pitch tracking data (for the years it exists) and adjust for important factors like pitcher, umpire, batter, and home-field advantage using a mixed-model approach. This grants us a number for how many strikes the catcher is personally adding to (or subtracting from) his pitchers' performance ... which we then convert to runs added or lost using linear weights.

Framing is one of the biggest parts of determining catcher value, but we also take into account blocking balls from going past, whether a scorer deems it a passed ball or a wild pitch. We use a similar approach–one that really benefits from the pitch tracking data that tells us what ends up in the dirt and what doesn't. We also include a catcher's ability to prevent stolen bases and how well they field balls in play, and *finally* we come up with our FRAA for catchers.

Pitching

Both pitching and fielding make up the half of baseball that isn't run scoring: run prevention. Separating pitching from fielding is a tough task, and most recent pitching analysis has branched off from Voros McCracken's famous (and controversial) statement, "There is little if any difference among major-league pitchers in their ability to prevent hits on balls hit in the field of play." The research of the analytic community has validated this to some extent, and there are a host of "defense-independent" pitching measures that have been developed to try and extricate the effect of the defense behind a hurler from the pitcher's work.

Our solution to this quandry is Deserved Run Average (DRA), our core pitching metric. DRA looks like earned run average (ERA), the tried-and-true pitching stat you've seen on every baseball broadcast or box score from the past century, but it's very different. To start, DRA takes an event-by-event look at what the pitchers does, and adjusts the value of that event based on different environmental factors like park, batter, catcher, umpire, base-out situation, run differential, inning, defense, home field advantage, pitcher role, and temperature. That mixed model gives us a pitcher's expected contribution, similar to what we do for our DRC+ model for hitters and FRAA model for catchers. (Oh, and we also consider the pitcher's effect on basestealing and on balls getting past the catcher.)

It's important to note that DRA is set to the scale of runs allowed per nine innings (RA9) instead of ERA, which makes DRA's scale slightly higher than ERA's. The reason for this is because ERA tends to overrate three types of pitchers:

1. Pitchers who play in parks where scorers hand out more errors. Official scorers differ significantly in the frequency at which they assign errors to fielders.
2. Ground-ball pitchers, because a substantial proportion of errors occur on grounders.
3. Pitchers who aren't very good. Better pitchers often allow fewer unearned runs than bad pitchers, because good pitchers tend to find ways to get out of jams.

Since the last time you picked up an edition of this book, we've also made a few minor changes to DRA to make it better. Recent research into "tunneling"–the act of throwing consecutive pitches that appear similar from a batter's point of view until after the swing decision point–data has given us a new contextual factor to account for in DRA: plate distance. This refers to the distance between successive pitches as they approach the plate, and while it has a smaller effect than factors like velocity or whiff rate, it still can help explain pitcher strikeout rate in our model.

New Pitching Metrics for 2019

We're including a few "new" pitching metrics for 2019's suite of Baseball Prospectus publications, but you may be familiar with them if you've spent time scouring the internet for stats.

Fastball Percentage

Our fastball percentage (FB%) statistic measures how frequently a pitcher throws a pitch classified as a "fastball," measured as a percentage of overall pitches thrown. We qualify three types of fastballs:

1. The traditional four-seam fastball;
2. The two-seam fastball or sinker;
3. "Hard cutters," which are pitches that have the movement profile of a cut fastball and are used as the pitcher's primary offering or in place of a more traditional fastball.

For example, a pitcher with a FB% of 67 throws any combination of these three pitches about two-thirds of the time.

Whiff Rate

Everybody loves a swing and a miss, and whiff rate (WHF) measures how frequently pitchers induce a swinging strike. To calculate WHF, we add up all the pitches thrown that ended with a swinging strike, then divide that number by a pitcher's total pitches thrown. Most often, high whiff rates correlate with high strikeout rates (and overall effective pitcher performance).

Called Strike Probability

Called Strike Probability (CSP) is a number that represents the likelihood that all of a pitcher's pitches will be called a strike while controlling for location, pitcher and batter handedness, umpire and count. Here's how it works: on each pitch, our model determines how many times (out of 100) that a similar pitch was called for a strike given those factors mentioned above, and when normalized for each batter's strike zone. Then we average the CSP for all pitches thrown by a pitcher in a season, and that gives us the yearly CSP percentage you see in the stats boxes.

As you might imagine, pitchers with a higher CSP are more likely to work in the zone, where pitchers with a lower CSP are likely locating their pitches outside the normal strike zone, for better or for worse.

Projections

Many of you aren't turning to this book just for a look at what a player has done, but for a look at what a player is going to do: the PECOTA projections. PECOTA, initially developed by Nate Silver (who has moved on to greater fame as a political analyst), consists of three parts:

1. Major-league equivalencies, which use minor-league statistics to project how a player will perform in the major leagues;
2. Baseline forecasts, which use weighted averages and regression to the mean to estimate a player's current true talent level; and
3. Aging curves, which uses the career paths of comparable players to estimate how a player's statistics are likely to change over time.

With all those important things covered, let's take a look at what's in the book this year.

Team Prospectus

You bought this book to learn more about your favorite (or maybe least-favorite, who are we to judge?) team, so let's talk about them. After a thoughtful preview of the 2019 season, you'll be presented with our Team Prospectus. This outlines many of the key statistics for each team's 2018 season, as well as a very inviting stadium diagram.

First you'll find the Performance Graphs page. The first is the 2018 Hit List Ranking. This shows our Hit List Rank for the team on each day of the 2018 season and is intended to give you a picture of the ups and downs of the team's season, including their highest and lowest ranks of the year. Hit List Rank measures overall team performance and drives the Hit List Power Rankings at the baseballprospectus.com website.

The second graph is Committed Payroll and helps you see how the team's payroll has compared to the MLB and divisional average payrolls over time. Payroll figures are currents as of January 1, 2019; with so many free agents still unsigned as of this writing, the final 2018 figure will likely be significantly different for many teams. (In the meantime, you can always find the most current data at Baseball Prospectus' Cot's Baseball Contracts page.)

Minnesota Twins 2019

The third graph is Farm System Ranking and displays how the Baseball Prospectus prospect team has ranked the organization's farm system since 2007. It also indicates the highest and lowest ranks that the farm system achieved over that time.

We start the Team Performance page with the squad's unadjusted and third-order 2018 win-loss records, presented in divisional context. We then list the three highest performing hitters and pitchers by WARP for 2018. Beneath that are a host of other team statistics. **Pythag** presents an adjusted 2018 winning percentage, calculated by taking runs scored per game (**RS/G**) and runs allowed per game (**RA/G**) for the team, and running them through a version of Bill James' Pythagorean formula that was refined and improved by David Smyth and Brandon Heipp. (The formula is called "Pythagenpat," which is equally fun to type and to say.)

Next up is **DRC+**, described earlier, to indicate the overall hitting ability of the team either above or below league-average. Run prevention on the pitching side is covered by **DRA** (also mentioned earlier) and another metric: Fielding Independent Pitching (**FIP**), which calculates another ERA-like statistic based on strikeouts, walks, and home runs recorded. Defensive Efficiency Rating (**DER**) tells us the percentage of balls in play turned into outs for the team, and is a quick fielding shorthand that rounds out run prevention.

After that, we have several measures related to roster composition, as opposed to on-field performance. **B-Age** and **P-Age** tell us the average age of a team's batters and pitchers, respectively. **Salary** is the combined team payroll for all on-field players, and Doug Pappas' Marginal Dollars per Marginal Win (**M$/MW**) tells us how much money a team spent to earn production above replacement level.

Ending this batch of statistics is the number of disabled list days a team had over the season (**DL Days**) and the amount of salary paid to players on the disabled list (**$ on DL**); this final number is expressed as a percentage of total payroll.

Next to each of these stats, we've listed each team's MLB rank in that category from 1st to 30th. In this, 1st always indicates a positive outcome and 30th a negative outcome, except in the case of salary–1st is highest.

The Team Projections page is intended to convey the team's operational capacity entering the 2019 season. We start with the team's PECOTA projected record for 2019, again in divisional context. The **+/-** column indicates how many more or less wins the team is projected to get than they got in 2018. We then list the three highest projected hitters and pitchers by WARP for 2018. A brief farm system summary follows, with the team's top prospect and number of BP Top 101 Prospects. Finally, we list the key new players and departed players, along with their 2019 projected WARP.

Alex Bregman 3B

Born: 03/30/94 Age: 25 Bats: R Throws: R
Height: 6'0" Weight: 180 Origin: Round 1, 2015 Draft (#2 overall)

YEAR	TEAM	LVL	AGE	PA	R	2B	3B	HR	RBI	BB	K	SB	CS	AVG/OBP/SLG
2016	CCH	AA	22	285	54	16	2	14	46	42	26	5	3	.297/.415/.559
2016	FRE	AAA	22	83	17	6	0	6	15	5	12	2	1	.333/.373/.641
2016	HOU	MLB	22	217	31	13	3	8	34	15	52	2	0	.264/.313/.478
2017	HOU	MLB	23	626	88	39	5	19	71	55	97	17	5	.284/.352/.475
2018	HOU	MLB	24	705	105	51	1	31	103	96	85	10	4	.286/.394/.532
2019	HOU	MLB	25	675	96	38	3	23	78	73	107	12	4	.272/.359/.463

Breakout: 6% Improve: 52% Collapse: 5% Attrition: 2% MLB: 100%
Comparables: Anthony Rendon, David Wright, Pablo Sandoval

YEAR	TEAM	LVL	AGE	PA	DRC+	VORP	BABIP	BRR	FRAA	WARP
2016	CCH	AA	22	285	172	38.9	.286	1.6	SS(51): -3.4, 3B(11): 1.4	2.7
2016	FRE	AAA	22	83	161	10.0	.333	-1.2	SS(14): 2.1, LF(3): -0.1	0.8
2016	HOU	MLB	22	217	107	9.6	.317	0.5	3B(40): 0.9, SS(6): -0.1	1.1
2017	HOU	MLB	23	626	114	34.7	.311	-1.5	3B(132): 8.7, SS(30): -2.9	3.9
2018	HOU	MLB	24	705	150	72.6	.289	-1.6	3B(136): 5.4, SS(28): -0.4	7.4
2019	HOU	MLB	25	675	125	37.3	.295	0.0	3B 7, SS 0	4.6

After the projections page, we share a few items about the team's home ballpark. There's the aforementioned diagram of the park's dimensions (including distances to the outfield wall), a few important biographical facts about the stadium, a graphic showing the height of the wall from the left-field pole to the right-field pole, and a table showing three-year park factors for the stadium. The park factors are displayed as indexes where 100 is average, 110 means that the park inflates the statistic in question by 10 percent, and 90 means that the park deflates the statistic in question by 10 percent.

Following the ballpark page, we have a **Personnel** section that lists many of the important decision-makers and upper-level field and operations staff members for the franchise, as well as any former Baseball Prospectus staff members who are currently part of the organization.

Position Players

After all that information and a thoughtful bylined essay covering each team, we present our player comments. Each player is listed with the major-league team who employed him as of early January 2019. If a player changed teams after that point via free agency, trade, or any other method, you'll be able to find them in the book for their previous squad.

First, we cover biographical information (age is as of June 30, 2019) before moving onto the stats themselves. Our statistic columns include standard identifying information like **YEAR**, **TEAM**, **LVL** (level of affiliated play) and **AGE** before getting into the numbers. Next, we provide raw, unstranslated numbers like you might find on the back of your dad's baseball cards: **PA** (plate appearances), **R** (runs), **2B** (doubles), **3B** (triples), **HR** (home runs), **RBI** (runs batted in), **BB** (walks), **K** (strikeouts), **SB** (stolen bases) and **CS** (caught stealing). Then we have unadjusted "slash" statistics: **AVG** (batting average), **OBP** (on-base percentage) and **SLG** (slugging percentage).

Just below the stats box is **PECOTA** data, which is discussed further in a following section. After that, it's on to a pithy and always-informative comment written by a member of the Baseball Prospectus staff, before we cover more stats.

The second text box repeats YEAR, TEAM, LVL, AGE, and PA, then moves on to **DRC+** (Deserved Runs Created Plus), which we described earlier as total offensive expected contribution compared to the league average. Next, one of our oldest active metrics, **VORP** (Value Over Replacement Player), considers offensive production, position and plate appearances. In essence, it is the number of runs contributed beyond what a replacement-level player at the same position would contribute if given the same percentage of team plate appearances. VORP does not consider the quality of a player's defense.

BABIP (batting average on balls in play) tells us how often a ball in play fell for a hit, and can help us identify whether a batter may have been lucky or not ... but note that high BABIPs also tend to follow the great hitters of our time, as well as speedy singles hitters who put the ball on the ground.

The next item is **BRR** (Baserunning Runs), which covers all of a player's baserunning accomplishments which includes (but isn't limited to) swiped bags and failed attempts. Next is **FRAA** (Fielding Runs Above Average), which also includes the number of games previously played at each position noted in parentheses. Multi-position players have only their two most frequent positions listed here, but their total FRAA number reflects all positions played.

Our last column here is **WARP** (Wins Above Replacement Player). WARP estimates the total value of a player, which means for hitters it takes into account hitting runs above average (calculated using the DRC+ model), BRR and FRAA. Then, it makes an adjustment for positions played and gives the player a credit for plate appearances based upon the difference between "replacement level"¬–which is derived from the quality of players added to a team's roster after the start of the season¬–and the league average.

Catchers

Catchers are a special breed, and thus they have earned their own separate box which displays some of the defensive metrics that we've built just for them. As an example, let's check out J.T. Realmuto.

YEAR	TEAM	P. COUNT	FRM RUNS	BLK RUNS	THRW RUNS	TOT RUNS
2016	MIA	18935	-8.5	1.8	2.1	-5.6
2017	MIA	18959	5.3	1.7	1.0	9.1
2018	MIA	16399	-0.4	0.9	0.1	0.4
2019	PHI	18448	-1.4	1.5	0.7	0.8

The **YEAR** and **TEAM** columns match what you'd find in the other stat box. **P. COUNT** indicates the number of pitches thrown while the catcher was behind the plate, including swinging strikes, fouls, and balls in play. **FRM RUNS** is the total run value the catcher provided (or cost) his team by influencing the umpire to call strikes where other catchers did not. **BLK RUNS** expresses the total run value above or below average for the catcher's ability to prevent wild pitches and passed balls. **THRW RUNS** is calculated using a similar model as the previous two statistics, and it measures a catcher's ability to throw out basestealers but also to dissuade them from testing his arm in the first place. It takes into account factors like the pitcher (including his delivery and pickoff move) and baserunner (who could be as fast as Billy Hamilton or as slow as Yonder Alonso). **TOT RUNS** is the sum of all of the previous three statistics.

Pitchers

Let's give our pitchers a turn, using 2018 NL Cy Young winner Jacob deGrom as our example. Take a look at his first stat block: the first line and the **YEAR**, **TEAM**, **LVL** and **AGE** columns are the same as in the position player example earlier.

Here too, we have a series of columns that display raw, unadjusted statistics compiled by the pitcher over the course of a season: **W** (wins), **L** (losses), **SV** (saves), **G** (games pitched), **GS** (games started), **IP** (innings pitched), **H** (hits allowed) and **HR** (home runs allowed). Next we have two statistics that are rates: **BB/9** (walks per nine innings) and **K/9** (strikeouts per nine innings), before returning to the unadjusted **K** (strikeouts).

Next up is **GB%** (ground ball percentage), which is the percentage of all batted balls that were hit in the ground, including both outs and hits. Remember, this is based on observational data and subject to human error, so please approach this with a healthy dose of skepticism.

BABIP (batting average on balls in play) is calculated using the same methodology as it is for position players, but it often tells us more about a pitcher than it does a hitter. With pitchers, a high BABIP is often due to poor defense or bad luck, and can often be an indicator of potential rebound, and a low BABIP may be cause to expect performance regression. (A typical league-average BABIP is close to .290-.300.)

After a witty 150ish words on the player like only Baseball Prospectus's staff can provide, it's on to that second stat block, which repeats the YEAR, TEAM, LVL, and AGE columns. The metrics **WHIP** (walks plus hits per inning pitched) and **ERA** (earned run average) are old standbys: WHIP measures walks and hits allowed on a per-inning basis, while ERA measures earned runs on a nine-inning basis. Neither of these stats are translated or adjusted.

DRA (Deserved Run Average) was described at length earlier, and measures how many runs the pitcher "deserved" to allow per nine innings. Please note that since we lack all the data points that would make for a "real" DRA for minor-league events, the DRA displayed for minor league partial-seasons is based off of different data. (That data is a modified version of our cFIP metric, which you can find more information about on our website.)

Jacob deGrom   RHP
Born: 06/19/88   Age: 31   Bats: L   Throws: R
Height: 6'4"   Weight: 180   Origin: Round 9, 2010 Draft (#272 overall)

YEAR	TEAM	LVL	AGE	W	L	SV	G	GS	IP	H	HR	BB/9	K/9	K	GB%	BABIP
2016	NYN	MLB	28	7	8	0	24	24	148	142	15	2.2	8.7	143	47%	.312
2017	NYN	MLB	29	15	10	0	31	31	201[1]	180	28	2.6	10.7	239	48%	.305
2018	NYN	MLB	30	10	9	0	32	32	217	152	10	1.9	11.2	269	48%	.281
2019	NYN	MLB	31	13	9	0	31	31	186	145	18	2.3	10.7	221	46%	.286

Breakout: 8%   Improve: 29%   Collapse: 28%   Attrition: 6%   MLB: 85%
Comparables: Erik Bedard, A.J. Burnett, CC Sabathia

YEAR	TEAM	LVL	AGE	WHIP	ERA	DRA	WARP	MPH	FB%	WHF	CSP
2016	NYN	MLB	28	1.20	3.04	3.30	3.5	96.3	59.6	12.1	47.2
2017	NYN	MLB	29	1.19	3.53	3.02	5.7	97.2	55.5	14.5	49.5
2018	NYN	MLB	30	0.91	1.70	2.09	8.0	98.2	52.1	16.3	48.4
2019	NYN	MLB	31	1.02	2.91	3.23	3.9	96.6	54.5	14.8	48.2

Just like with hitters, **WARP** (Wins Above Replacement Player) is a total value metric that puts pitchers of all stripes on the same scale as position players. We use DRA as the primary input for our calculation of WARP. You might notice that relief pitchers (due to their limited innings) may have a lower WARP than you were expecting or than you might see in other WARP-like metrics. WARP does not take leverage into account, just the actions a pitcher performs and the expected value of those actions ... which ends up judging high-leverage relief pitchers differently than you might imagine given their prestige and market value.

MPH gives you the pitcher's 95th percentile velocity for the noted season, in order to give you an idea of what the *peak* fastball velocity a pitcher possesses. Since this comes from our pitch tracking data, it is not publicly available for minor-league pitchers.

Finally, we display the three new pitching metrics we described earlier. **FB%** (fastball percentage) gives you the percentage of fastballs thrown out of all pitches. **WhiffRt** (whiff rate) tells you the percentage of swinging strikes induced out of all pitches. **CS Prob** (called strike probability) expresses the likelihood of all pitches thrown to result in a called strike, after controlling for factors like handedness, umpire, pitch type, count, and location.

PECOTA

All players have PECOTA projections for 2019, as well as a set of other numbers that describe the performance of comparable players according to PECOTA. All projections for 2019 are for the player at the date we went to press in early January and are projected into the league and park context as indicated by the team abbreviation. All PECOTA projected statistics represent a player's projected major-league performance.

The numbers beneath the player's stats–Breakout, Improve, Collapse, Attrition–are part and parcel of the PECOTA projections. They estimate the likelihood of changes in performance relative to the player's previously-established level of production, based on the performance of comparable players:

Breakout Rate is the percent change that a player's production will improve by at least 20 percent relative to the weighted average of his performance over his most recent seasons.

Improve Rate is the percent chance that a player's production will improve at all relative to his baseline performance. A player who is expected to perform just the same as he has in the recent past will have an Improve Rate of 50 percent.

Collapse Rate is the percent chance that a position player's production will decline by at least 25 percent relative to his baseline performance.

Attrition Rate operates on playing time rather than performance. Specifically, it measures the likelihood that a player's playing time will decrease by at least 50 percent relative to his established level.

Breakout Rate and Collapse Rate can sometimes be counterintuitive for players who have already experienced a radical change in performance level. It's also worth noting that the projected decline in a player's rate performances might not be indicative of an expected decline in underlying ability or skill, but could just be an anticipated correction following a breakout season.

MLB% is the percentage of similar players who played in the major leagues in their relevant season.

The final pieces of information are the player's three highest-scoring comparable players as determined by PECOTA. All comparables represent a snapshot of how the listed player was performing at the same age as the current player, so if a 23-year-old pitcher is compared to Bartolo Colon, he's actually being compared to a 23-year-old Colon, not the version that pitched for the Rangers in 2018, nor to Colon's career as a whole.

Minnesota Twins 2019

A few points about pitcher projections. First, we aren't yet projecting peak velocity, so that column will be blank in the PECOTA lines. Second, projecting DRA is trickier than evaluating past performance, because it is unclear how deserving each pitcher will be of his anticipated outcomes. However, we know that another DRA-related statistic–contextual FIP or cFIP–estimates future run scoring very well. So for PECOTA, the projected DRA figures you see are based on the past cFIPs generated by the pitcher and comparable players over time, along with the other factors described above.

Lineouts

In each chapter's Lineouts section, you'll find abbreviated text comments, as well as most of same information you'd find in our full player comments. We limit the stats boxes in this section to only including the 2018 information for each player.

Exclusive Player Visualizations

In our constant battle to provide you with new and interesting baseball content you can't find anywhere else, we've added a trio of data visualizations to each hitter's entry in these books and a pair of visualizations for each pitcher.

For hitters, you'll find three new infographics. The first is each player's **Batted Ball Distribution**, which displays the five major sections of the field: LF (left), LCF (left center), CF (center), RCF (right center), and RF (right). The percentage indicated tells us what percentage of batted balls from that hitter fell within that part of the field during the 2018 season. We've also included the hitter's slugging percentage on balls in play (also called **SLGCON**) for that part of the field.

You'll also see two heatmaps: **Strike Zone vs LHP** and **Strike Zone vs RHP**. These heat maps represent a view of the strike zone from behind the catcher. Areas where there is a darker coloration represent the places where a higher percentage of pitches resulted in hits. In other words, the heatmap represents a hitter's "sweet spots" for getting hits against either left-handed or right-handed pitchers, depending on the image.

Pitchers get two images that help explain what their pitches look like from a hitter's perspective: **Pitch Shape vs LHH** and **Pitch Shape vs RHH**. These images show you the shape and the "tunneling" effect of each pitcher's offerings from the batter's perspective. For each type of pitch that a pitcher throws (represented by an indicator shape), there's a set of dots indicating the flight path, where each dot represents a 0.01-second interval. This maps the average trajectory and speed of an offering, ending where the ball crosses the plate. The solid black box represents the regular strike zone, while the gray contour lines indicate the range of locations that a pitcher typically works in.

Below the image, we provide a bit more detailed information about each pitcher's average offering in the **Pitch Types** box. Here, we also list each of the pitcher's major offerings under the **Type** column.

- **Fastballs** (which usually refers to the four-seam variation)
- **Sinkers** and/or two-seam fastballs
- **Cutters** (which could include "hard" cutters like cut fastballs and "soft" cutters that resemble hard sliders)
- **Changeups** (not including most splitters)
- **Splitters** (split-fingered pitches, forkballs, and some split-changes)
- **Sliders** and/or slurves
- **Curveballs** (including spike-curveballs and knuckle-curveballs, as well as some slurvy curves)
- **Slow curveballs** and/or eephus pitches
- **Knuckleballs**
- **Screwballs**

The **Freq** column indicates the percentage of overall pitches that fall into each of those type categories; if a pitcher has a 16.55% score for changeups, then that's the percent of all pitches that he throws as changeups. **Velo** is exactly what you think it is: the average miles per hour for each pitch type. **H Mov** is the number of inches of horizontal movement on the average pitch of that type, while **V Mov** is the number of inches of vertical movement on the average pitch of that type. (At Baseball Prospectus, we measure this over the long flight of the ball and include gravity into the V Mov number in order to give you the most realistic representation of what the pitch *actually* does.)

If you're wondering about the second number in brackets, that's the index for that velocity or movement compared to the league average. Like DRC+, a score of 100 means that the speed or movement is about the same as league average, while a higher score means that there's higher velocity or movement than the league average. Numbers below 100 indicate less velocity or movement than the league average.

Part 1: Team Analysis

Table for Two: Previewing the 2019 Minnesota Twins

Mike Bates and Aaron Gleeman

MIKE BATES: For a team that's made quite a few moves this offseason, including a pretty big one in signing Nelson Cruz, doesn't the Twins' offseason feel a little incomplete?

AARON GLEEMAN: Definitely. Their moves (or lack of moves) can be described in a lot of different ways, some good and some bad, but the overriding feeling I get looking at the entire picture today is… unfinished. Or maybe just incomplete, like you said, since I'm not sure there are any plans to finish it. They started by making some shrewd bargain pickups for the lineup in Jonathan Schoop and C.J. Cron, then made the big splash with Cruz, and then… nothing.

It seems odd that a team would spend $14 million on a 38-year-old designated hitter only to spend a total of $5 million on pitching help in the form of Blake Parker and Martin Perez. It feels like 75 percent of a plan that was supposed to include a trade or two for an impact arm, or at least the signing of, say, Gio Gonzalez or Charlie Morton or Joakim Soria. Something. They have a clear need, they have all kinds of money to spend, they have the offense in place to compete on that side of the ball. It's confusing.

And the fact that their current payroll sits at $105 million, nearly $25 million below last year's mark, makes it even more frustrating.

MIKE: Especially since this would not be remotely close to the first time a Twins team pinched pennies while pocketing millions in revenue instead of reinvesting it. Calvin Griffith refused to pursue free agents or to re-sign young stars on the cusp of entering the open market. Carl Pohlad kept payrolls low after the strike in 1994 and even worked with Bud Selig to try to contract the franchise in 2002 for a windfall payment. It's just that, this time, the rest of the league seems to be doing exactly the same thing at exactly the same time. The Twins are at least no longer outliers in their frugality.

But, to be fair, I think we both believe Derek Falvey and Thad Levine are smart executives and are building a strong front office staff, which is a massive improvement over where the club was when it began this underwhelming stretch in 2011. And, because of that, while no one can deny Byron Buxton and Miguel Sano have underperformed, I have to assume there's a plan beyond what

Falvey has said publicly—that they "need that group to take steps forward" and the implication that they're waiting to see what happens before making moves to shore up the rotation and bullpen.

That just seems so passive. I mean, if and when Buxton (.234/.297/.390, 85 DRC+, 2.0 WARP) and Sano (.235/.326/.429, 106 DRC+, 1.8 WARP) beat their projections, as constructed the Twins are still probably on the outside looking in on a Wild Card race, aren't they?

AARON: To me, if you truly think you're a Sano/Buxton return to form away from being a legit playoff contender, then you'd make even more of an effort to beef up the rest of the roster. Like you, I have a great deal of confidence in this front office and the coaching, development, and analytics staffs they've built, and I absolutely think this team is in a better place now than it was five years ago. But none of that should have precluded them from investing another $25 million in pitching help for this season.

Building something for the long term doesn't mean you can't also put a better product on the field in the short term. And to put the team's lack of pitching additions at the feet of Buxton and Sano seems self-defeating, or at least seems to set them up to take the brunt of criticism if the team underperforms. PECOTA has the Twins right at .500, and I think that's reasonable. I'd probably say 82-85 wins, as opposed to 81, in part because I think the bottom three teams in the AL Central are still going to be truly awful, but this is certainly a mediocre team on paper.

I've gone back and forth on this over the last couple years, but I'm now more confident in Buxton being a consistently excellent player than Sano, who's going to have to hit for a massive amount of power to make up for the other flaws in his game. Buxton just needs to stay healthy and hit even a little bit, and he's an All-Star. If you're picking a breakout player for 2019, who do you go with? I'll say Buxton, because I always say Buxton, with a nod to Fernando Romero on the pitching side if they can get him into a role he's comfortable with.

MIKE: Buxton would be my choice as well, although one could argue he already broke out in 2017 before last year's injury-caused debacle. The defense and baserunning are so elite that, as you said, even a mediocre performance at the plate is going to make him one of the best center fielders in baseball. I would have been more excited about Romero's potential if they were going to leave him in the rotation, but that seems unlikely now. He'll be effective in a relief role, especially one that allows him to throw multiple innings at a time, but there's something of a ceiling to the value a reliever can provide.

Like everyone else, I keep waiting on Max Kepler's performance to catch up to his tools and athleticism. He's 26 now, so he may be what he's going to ultimately be, unfortunately, which is a streaky hitter best used in a platoon role. However, in November our own Matthew Trueblood pointed out that Kepler may have turned a corner toward the end of 2018 and his defense remains excellent in a corner spot. If he can manage to even hit like an average right fielder, he's going to be exceptionally valuable. The Twins seem to agree, having locked Kepler up for the next five-plus seasons for $35 million.

I'll also put in for Jorge Polanco, whom the Twins also extended this spring for at least five years and $25 million. He's now a year removed from a PED suspension and is going to, hopefully, only spend half a year at shortstop before transitioning to second base in favor of Nick Gordon. PECOTA isn't high on Polanco, but the Twins sure are. Like them, I'm inclined to believe he's poised to build on his success at the plate last year and would be a strong defender at second base.

Speaking of Gordon, the Twins have built a very impressive farm system, and that's one of the reasons they seem to feel they're trapped between this core and the next. Assuming more help is not coming from outside the organization, do you see anyone else coming up to make an impact for them in 2019?

AARON: I think Polanco will eventually wind up at second base, but it'll probably be because of Royce Lewis and not Gordon. Almost everyone I've talked to in the prospect realm is really down on Gordon, and he was pretty brutal at Triple-A last season. He's too young to give up on and a good half-season at Triple-A could get him to the majors, but I no longer think the Twins are making their plans around him. If not for his former draft status and his MLB family, he'd be just another mid-level prospect.

They have quite a few prospects—and recent graduates, like Romero—who should get a look at some point this season. Some we've already seen a bit, like Stephen Gonsalves and Kohl Stewart, but also Gordon, Brent Rooker, Lewis Thorpe, LaMonte Wade. But those aren't the system's headliners, and barring something unexpected Lewis, Alex Kirilloff, and Brusdar Graterol—who each ranked among BP's top 50 prospects—have a 2020 (or 2021) ETA.

I don't necessarily think this year's call-ups are going to dramatically improve the team. If anything, if there are a bunch of prospects in the majors come June or July that probably means things haven't gone particularly well for the Twins. Which, again, is why their lack of offseason pitching additions confused me so much. It's not as if they're biding time until the arrivals of elite prospects. The next "wave" is a bunch of potential back-of-the-rotation starters and middle relievers, and that's coming from someone who's warmed to Stewart quite a bit.

MIKE: So, if there isn't any help of note coming from within, and Falvey and Levine refuse to bring in help through the free agent market, it seems to me that 2019 is poised to be a big missed opportunity. That will not sit well with a fan base that has largely been asked to be patient since 2011. That said, there are a lot of things to like about this Twins team. Assuming Buxton can stay healthy, the outfield defense should go back to being the best in baseball. And that will only help the rotation, which is probably the strongest the team's had since 2008.

Jose Berrios has developed into a strong no. 2 starter and is still only 25. Kyle Gibson turned a corner toward the end of 2017 by moving to the far edge of the pitching rubber and focusing on his four-seam fastball, becoming one of the few pitchers to actually start to throw harder after turning 30. Speaking of hard throwers, Michael Pineda was a shrewd pickup last offseason who should fully recover from Tommy John surgery to be a competent mid-rotation starter, and Jake Odorizzi is perfectly serviceable in the fourth slot. I'm curious to see what they're going to do for a fifth starter. Martin Perez, who hasn't been worth more than one WARP since 2013, doesn't inspire a ton of confidence.

AARON: I definitely think the fan base is, I dunno, let's call it cranky. And for good reason, I think, although lots of that "good reason" was due to the previous regime. On the day the Twins signed Cruz, there was a ton of excitement. Fans thought it was a signal that, in addition to putting their hopes into the long-term outlook, they'd have a contender to watch in 2019. And maybe even more than that, it felt like an indication this front office would truly be different than the previous one. And then… nothing.

You sign Cruz and follow that up with a couple impact pitching moves, and the entire tone of this preview could have changed. Twins Twitter would be ripping PECOTA for underrating the team's chances. And no one would be talking about payroll at all. I think that's fair—I'll gladly lead the charge about this offseason being a half-measure and/or a missed opportunity—but I also think the 2019 team still figures to be pretty decent. They have a not-unreasonable chance to make the playoffs, if the Indians come back to the pack a bit or the second Wild Card is available for 85-88 wins. But because there's such an obvious sense of things not done, or a job not completed, that overshadows the positives.

MIKE: And I'd put them around 84-86 wins, by which I mean we are essentially agreed. PECOTA's dim take on Buxton and Sano feels wrong to me, given that it can't take into account all of the context for their struggles last year, and I think they'll each be worth three wins or better, perhaps significantly better in Buxton's case. That said, I do think the team will have trouble getting that second Wild Card simply because one of the A's, Angels, or Rays will win 87 or more. And that feels right, both analytically and karmically.

AARON: I'll stick with 82-85 wins, which is both slightly more optimistic than PECOTA and slightly less optimistic than the Vegas over/under.

Performance Graphs

2018 Hit List Ranking

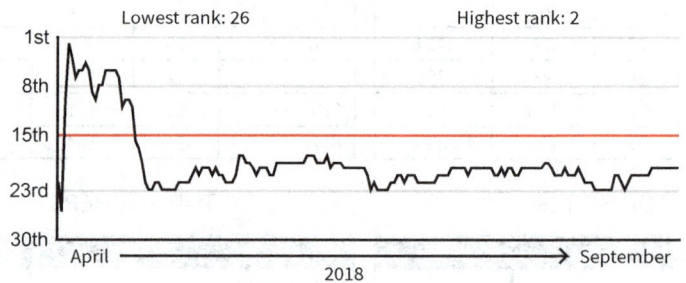

Committed Payroll (in millions)

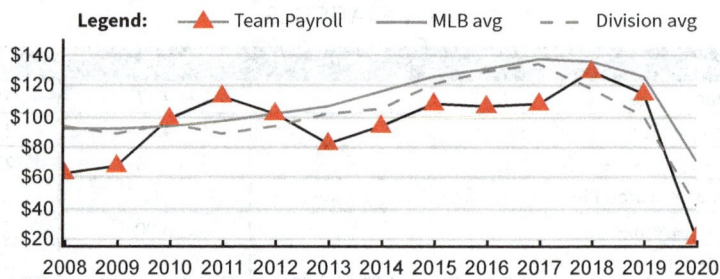

Farm System Ranking

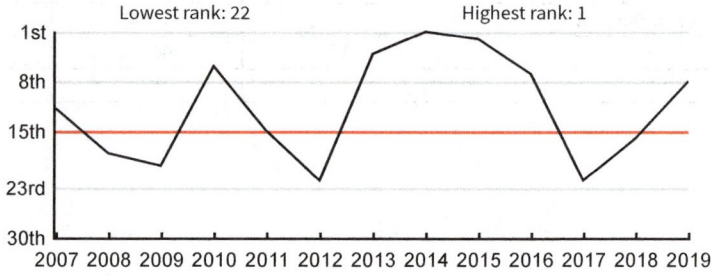

2018 Team Performance

ACTUAL STANDINGS

Team	W	L	Pct
CLE	91	71	.561
MIN	**78**	**84**	**.481**
DET	64	98	.395
CHA	62	100	.382
KCA	58	104	.358

THIRD-ORDER STANDINGS

Team	W	L	Pct
CLE	92	70	.567
MIN	**70**	**92**	**.432**
DET	62	100	.382
CHA	61	101	.376
KCA	58	104	.358

TOP HITTERS

Player	WARP
Eddie Rosario	3.6
Max Kepler	2.9
Byron Buxton	1.3

TOP PITCHERS

Player	WARP
Kyle Gibson	2.5
Jose Berrios	2.4
Fernando Romero	1.4

VITAL STATISTICS

Statistic Name	Value	Rank
Pythagenpat	.477	18th
Runs Scored per Game	4.56	13th
Runs Allowed per Game	4.78	22nd
Deserved Runs Created Plus	95	17th
Deserved Run Average	5.00	24th
Fielding Independent Pitching	4.42	22nd
Defensive Efficiency Rating	.698	25th
Batter Age	28.2	18th
Pitcher Age	28.1	15th
Salary	$128.7M	18th
Marginal $ per Marginal Win	$3.9M	15th
Disabled List Days	$966.0M	11th
$ on DL	21%	25th

2019 Team Projections

PROJECTED STANDINGS

Team	W	L	Pct	+/-
CLE	97	65	.598	+6
MIN	**82**	**80**	**.506**	**+4**
KCA	72	90	.444	+14
CHA	70	92	.432	+8
DET	67	95	.413	+3

TOP PROJECTED HITTERS

Player	WARP
Nelson Cruz	3.3
C.J. Cron	2.2
Byron Buxton	2.1

TOP PROJECTED PITCHERS

Player	WARP
Jose Berrios	3.1
Kyle Gibson	1.9
Taylor Rogers	0.7

FARM SYSTEM REPORT

Top Prospect	Number of Top 101 Prospects
Royce Lewis, #8	3

KEY DEDUCTIONS

Player	WARP
Robbie Grossman	1.1
Logan Forsythe	0.5

KEY ADDITIONS

Player	WARP
Nelson Cruz	3.3
C.J. Cron	2.2
Jonathan Schoop	2.0
Marwin Gonzalez	1.6
Lucas Duda	0.8
Martin Perez	0.6
Blake Parker	0.4

Team Personnel

EVP, Chief Baseball Officer
Derek Falvey

SVP, General Manager
Thad Levine

Assistant General Manager
Rob Antony

VP, Player Personnel
Mike Radcliff

Manager
Rocco Baldelli

BP Alumni
Ezra Wise

Target Field Stats

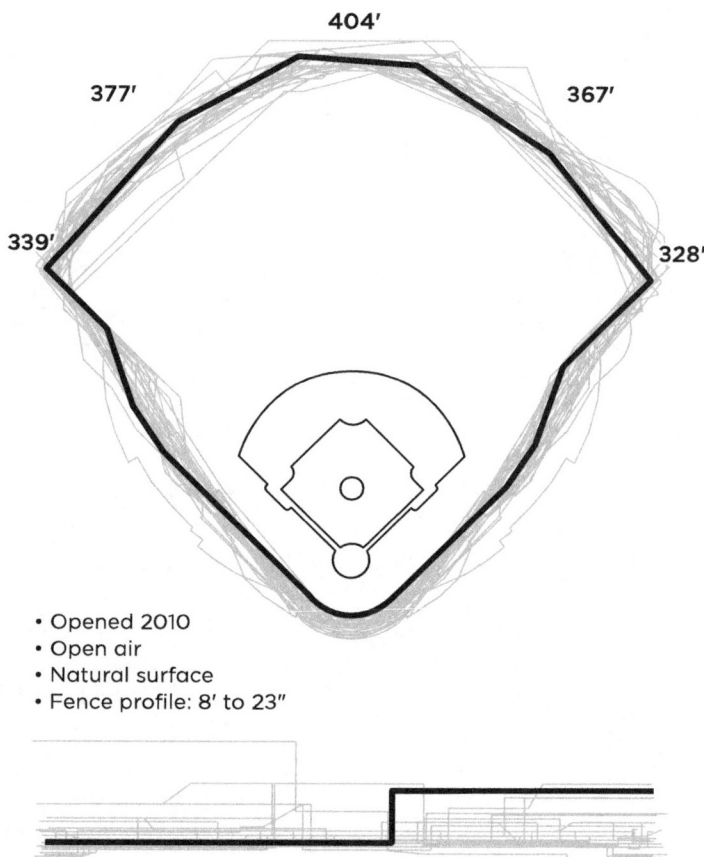

- Opened 2010
- Open air
- Natural surface
- Fence profile: 8' to 23"

Three-Year Park Factors

Runs	Runs/RH	Runs/LH	HR/RH	HR/LH
101	101	100	102	98

Twins Team Analysis

Early on the morning of December 12, 2010, the roof of the Metrodome ripped open and gave way beneath the weight of a blizzard's heavy snow accumulation, which might be the most uniquely "Minnesota sports" thing that has ever happened. Caught on video by a news camera left running overnight, it was an astounding sight to behold.

A writeup in the *Minneapolis Star Tribune* described the aftermath: "Inside the bitterly cold stadium Sunday morning, a surreal scene emerged: Sunshine shimmered on seats and splattered snow covered the green turf. Lights and giant speakers hung perilously low above the field."

The Twins had called that giant inflated marshmallow home for 28 years before relocating across downtown in the spring. For baseball fans in a football-dominated market, there was a certain schadenfreude in seeing such misfortune fall upon the Vikings, who remained hapless inhabitants of The Dome.

Two months earlier, the Twins had capped their inaugural season at Target Field, a blissfully roofless marvel that instantly joined the ranks of baseball's finest yards. Yep, things were lookin' up for the Twins, fresh off their second straight American League Central title with a sparkling new ballpark, the reigning Manager of the Year in Ron Gardenhire and—most importantly—four-time All-Star catcher Joe Mauer locked up for many years to come.

Little did the Twins know they were about to experience their own deflating collapse.

In 2011, Gardenhire saw his team's win total drop from 94 to 63. As injuries and setbacks piled up, the roof caved in on the once-admired franchise, burying them under an ever-rising avalanche. That's more or less been the story of the past eight years, during which the Twins went 570-726 (.440) with zero division titles after going 708-589 (.546) with five division titles in the previous eight seasons. Minnesota has the worst record in baseball since 2011.

Any of the following names and terms are liable to trigger Twins fans who've seen their beautiful ballpark blighted by so much ugly baseball: *Matt Capps, pitch to contact, Tsuyoshi Nishioka, bilateral leg weakness, Total System Failure.* And last season, we saw another phrase added to this field of disdainful distinction: *This is how we baseball.*

The team's grammatically painful marketing slogan drew plenty of Twitter guffaws when unveiled in the spring, but quickly became more sad than funny as the backdrop for a season full of grim developments and unmet promise. The

Minnesota Twins 2019

Twins baseballed their way to a sub-.500 record in a division where three teams lost 98 or more games. After surging to a Wild Card spot in 2017, the freshly remodeled front office pumped record payroll into supplementing its electrifying young core with veteran free agent help, and then that core just…fizzled.

When Paul Molitor managed the Twins to 85 wins in 2017, sneaking into the postseason ever so briefly, it was primarily on the strength of five key contributors who combined for 16.3 WARP: Joe Mauer, Brian Dozier, Byron Buxton, Miguel Sano, Ervin Santana. In 2018, those same five players returned to produce 1.3 WARP for the Twins, with Mauer's miniscule 0.7 WARP ranking as the best of the sad bunch. That's the story in a nutshell. Given this astonishing drop-off, it's actually a minor miracle the team won 78 games last season. It wasn't enough to save Molitor, who was dismissed shortly after the season. The soft-spoken, cerebral skipper hadn't done much to merit firing—tribulations erased any chance at a successful outcome in 2018—but he also hadn't done much to merit keeping around, either.

A notoriously stable and loyal outfit, the Twins saw remarkably little churn in the quarter-century following their last championship in 1991. So when Gardenhire got the axe in 2014 following a fourth straight 90-loss season, it was a surprise. And when institutional general manager Terry Ryan was ousted two years later, in the wake of a 103-loss catastrophe, it came as a full-on shock to the system. But not necessarily the bad kind. More like the awakening, invigorating jolt of leaping into Lake Superior's chilly October embrace.

The Twins finally shook off insularity and embraced the game's changing tide. In a 180-degree pivot (a polar plunge?), they replaced the 62-year-old Ryan with 33-year-old Derek Falvey, plucked out of Cleveland's hotbed front office. Tossing out the old playbook, Minnesota created a new position for Falvey (chief baseball officer) and let him hire his own general manager, (Thad Levine, previously Jon Daniels' right-hand man in Texas). They've since dramatically expanded the research and development department, investing heavily in an area the previous regime viewed largely as an annoyance.

Of course, you can't put lipstick on a pig, and you can't just slap a new roof on a dingy, dilapidated Dome and call it good. The Vikings did replace and re-inflate the Metrodome's Teflon canopy, spending a couple more years in its confines, but ultimately they recognized what needed to be done: They tore down the entire dated structure and built anew in its place. That patch of land is now occupied by U.S. Bank Stadium, which is either a world-class entertainment venue or a billion-dollar eyesore depending on who you ask.

Similarly, revamping the Twins' baseball operations department was only the first step in a rebuild from the ground up. Molitor was deeply ingrained in the organization before taking over, as much a vestige of the past as his well-tenured veteran clubhouse stalwarts Dozier, Santana, and Mauer. Each moved on after 2018. Only one, however, was the subject of tearful on-field tributes.

Mauer was the face of Twins baseball, for better or worse. The locally sourced no. 1 overall draft pick blossomed into an MVP in his own backyard—a storybook tale of the modern era, complete with hideous comments section. The 2018 season was filled with milestones for the 15-year veteran, wrapping up his $184 million mega-deal, but still he was treated by many as a millstone. His hefty salary, lack of prototypical power and "aw shucks" personality made Mauer a magnet for misguided vitriol from fans, columnists and radio hosts alike.

No, he didn't hit many home runs. And if you called him milquetoast, he'd think you were talking about his favorite late-night snack. But whether or not you could revel in Mauer's unbridled Minnesotan docility, any true baseball diehard had to appreciate the absolute skill and precision with which he played the game. His smooth lefty swing was picture perfect, as if conjured into existence by an overzealous hitting coach. From his first day in the majors to his last, he understood the strike zone better than most umpires. He was as clutch as they come, retiring with the second-highest active batting average in RISP situations, behind only Joey Votto. Mauer played Gold Glove-caliber defense at catcher, and then, after a concussion forced him away from the position, he played Gold Glove-caliber defense at first base.

By the end, he wasn't producing much all-around value. That 2013 brain injury was a costly one for Mauer the player, turning him from elite catcher to middling first baseman and throwing a surefire Hall of Fame career drastically off course. In five years at first base, he produced a total of just 0.2 WARP more than he did in his final season at catcher alone. Yet for us hopeless purists, he remained a joy to watch until the very end. "The man was born to play baseball," tweeted teammate Mitch Garver shortly after an emotional 2018 season finale that saw Mauer suit up and receive one last pitch as catcher in the ninth inning.

Garver was the first rookie catcher for Minnesota since Mauer to give real cause for intrigue, posting a .749 OPS in 102 games after an outstanding 2017 season at Triple-A. He's among a new-look wave of talent that hopes to lead Minnesota back to the promised land; a youth-fueled group with a youthful new leader—Rocco Baldelli is now MLB's youngest manager, and Falvey and Levine are betting that the 37-year-old, fished out of Tampa's ranks, can take this talent-laden roster he's inheriting to the next level.

Unfortunately, Garver was one of the few on that roster to inspire much confidence last season. There were others, like Jose Berrios, Eddie Rosario, Jake Cave, Kyle Gibson and Taylor Rogers, but too many stumbled and scuffled—most vitally Buxton and Sano, two of the Twins' most critical assets. Each endured a nightmare season derailed by injuries, performance regressions and friction with the front office. It's hard to have much faith in Minnesota's short-term viability with that duo wandering by the wayside, but then it's also hard to forget the game-changing ability each displayed only one year earlier.

In 2017, Sano was an All-Star slugger and Buxton was among baseball's most valuable second-half contributors, winning a Gold Glove in center field. They're still young (both 25 as of Opening Day) and each possesses a signature skill—Sano's raw power, Buxton's straightaway speed—ranking at the highest of percentiles. Those are building-block tools for building-block players, and if the reconstruction of the Twins as a contender is to happen in short order, they'll need to bear weight.

Buxton and Sano are both down and out coming off campaigns more or less ruined by physical issues. Baldelli, whose own promising career was sabotaged by a rare muscle fatigue disorder, knows a thing or two about being at the helpless mercy of one's health. Perhaps he can bring to the table a relatability beyond that "under 45, recently retired" status now so in vogue around the league. He made a point to visit both Buxton and Sano for face-to-face meetings this offseason, traveling first to Georgia and then to the Dominican Republic in the hopes of getting to know his star pupils in a way Molitor never seemed to.

Cutting-edge trends are now guiding the Twins organization, a direct departure from the previous norm. The coupling of Falvey and Baldelli as figureheads creates strong parallels with Andy MacPhail and Tom Kelly, who took over as Minnesota's GM/manager duo in the mid-1980s, at even younger ages than the new regime. MacPhail and Kelly teamed up to win two World Series championships with a young core that blossomed together.

They also built an infrastructure that lasted three decades and yielded plenty of success, even if the final years were marked by decay. Now, the franchise fully presses restart, with fresh leadership and new faces all over the roster (including Nelson Cruz, the club's big-ticket offseason addition). Lying ahead is a potentially rapid rebuild, depending on the resilience of those entrenched foundational pieces and the speed at which the next big wave of talent—top-50 prospects Royce Lewis, Brusdar Graterol and Alex Kirilloff—can join them in the majors.

It's funny how history repeats itself. Granted, not as funny as the Vikings having to play a "home game" in Detroit.

—*Nick Nelson is a writer at Twins Daily.*

Part 2: Player Analysis

Minnesota Twins 2019

Ehire Adrianza   UT
Born: 08/21/89   Age: 29   Bats: B   Throws: R
Height: 6'1"   Weight: 170   Origin: International Free Agent, 2006

YEAR	TEAM	LVL	AGE	PA	R	2B	3B	HR	RBI	BB	K	SB	CS	AVG/OBP/SLG
2016	SFN	MLB	26	71	3	2	0	2	7	2	13	0	1	.254/.299/.381
2017	ROC	AAA	27	44	1	0	0	0	3	6	11	0	1	.216/.326/.216
2017	MIN	MLB	27	186	30	9	2	2	24	16	25	8	1	.265/.324/.383
2018	MIN	MLB	28	366	42	23	1	6	39	24	82	5	1	.251/.301/.379
2019	MIN	MLB	29	93	10	4	0	2	9	7	19	2	1	.241/.304/.361

Breakout: 13%   Improve: 48%   Collapse: 9%   Attrition: 24%   MLB: 94%
Comparables: Brendan Ryan, Cliff Pennington, Jason Bartlett

Of the nine previous write-ups Adrianza has gotten in these pages, nine have used the exact phrases "good-glove/no-hit" or "utility player." That's a failure of imagination, an affliction Adrianza himself has nobly avoided. Over pieces of six big-league seasons, he's slowly organized an approach aimed at generating the consistent loft and authoritative contact on which hinge his chances of moving beyond those labels and into the realm of the regulars. Alas, he's not up to it. As he's more often generated what passes for high-value contact, he's lost the ability to draw walks and put the ball in play at an elite rate. Worse, the drives he does lift don't fly the way he imagines they might. Too many land relatively harmlessly in gloves or gaps, rather than bleachers. He's no longer so slick afield as to risk being called "good-glove," either.

YEAR	TEAM	LVL	AGE	PA	DRC+	VORP	BABIP	BRR	FRAA	WARP
2016	SFN	MLB	26	71	82	0.9	.292	-0.8	SS(13): 0.8, 2B(7): 0.3	0.1
2017	ROC	AAA	27	44	73	-1.5	.308	-0.1	LF(4): 1.0, SS(2): 0.3	0.0
2017	MIN	MLB	27	186	87	6.2	.291	1.6	SS(29): 3.0, LF(17): 1.5	1.1
2018	MIN	MLB	28	366	82	7.6	.313	0.7	SS(64): -6.1, 3B(28): 0.6	0.0
2019	MIN	MLB	29	93	87	1.8	.289	0.1	SS 0, 3B 0	0.2

Ehire Adrianza, continued

Batted Ball Distribution

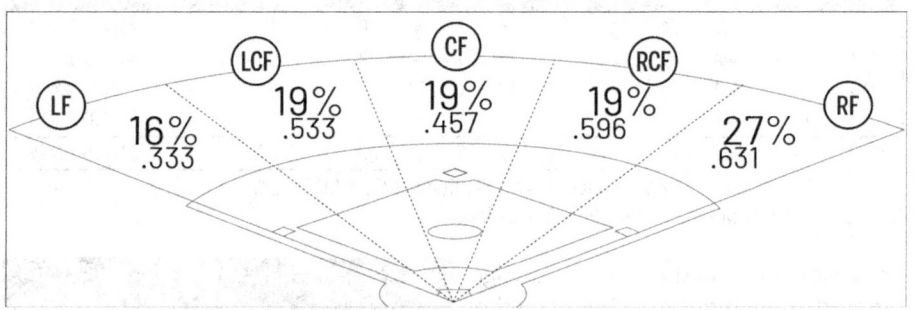

Strike Zone vs LHP   **Strike Zone vs RHP**

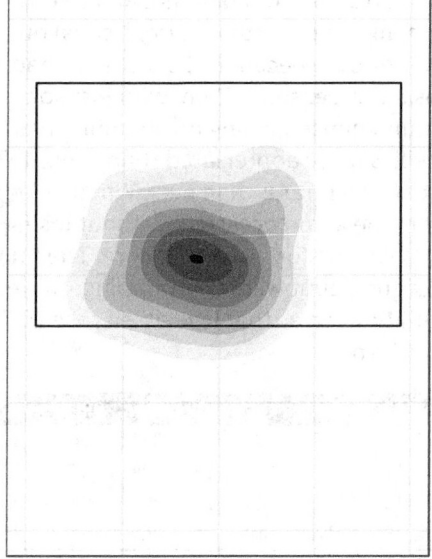

Willians Astudillo   C/UT

Born: 10/14/91   Age: 27   Bats: R   Throws: R
Height: 5'9"   Weight: 225   Origin: International Free Agent, 2008

YEAR	TEAM	LVL	AGE	PA	R	2B	3B	HR	RBI	BB	K	SB	CS	AVG/OBP/SLG
2016	MIS	AA	24	342	24	9	0	4	30	5	11	1	1	.267/.293/.332
2017	RNO	AAA	25	128	22	14	0	4	22	4	5	0	1	.342/.370/.558
2018	ROC	AAA	26	307	30	17	1	12	38	10	14	7	4	.276/.314/.469
2018	MIN	MLB	26	97	9	4	1	3	21	2	3	0	0	.355/.371/.516
2019	MIN	MLB	27	188	21	12	0	6	22	7	20	1	1	.260/.298/.429

Breakout: 7%   Improve: 39%   Collapse: 4%   Attrition: 37%   MLB: 66%
Comparables: Jose Morales, Tomas Telis, Steve Clevenger

YEAR	TEAM	P. COUNT	FRM RUNS	BLK RUNS	THRW RUNS	TOT RUNS
2017	RNO	2571	1.4	0.0	-0.2	1.0
2018	MIN	2234	1.1	0.5	0.0	1.6
2018	ROC	5149	1.4	0.3	0.3	1.6
2019	MIN	3484	0.4	0.1	0.0	0.6

For years, the man they call La Tortuga labored anonymously, buffeted by the breaks of the game, flipped onto his metaphorical shell time and time again. He was overlooked and underrated — out of mind, and often (thanks to persistent injury issues) out of sight. He became a baseball nomad, plodding through three organizations in as many seasons. Then, with just some good health and a slight adjustment, he found himself taking off. Astudillo has always been a good pitch framer; that skill is more appreciated than ever. He's always been a singular contact hitter; that skill is rarer than ever. When he added the ability to hit the ball hard and get it in the air on occasion, without losing that extraordinary ability to avoid whiffs, he became too good to ignore. The numbers he put up during his brief big-league debut were eye-popping. His level of popularity rose to meet that of his utility, even as that level itself rose. He's not a turtle, really. He's just a fat, slow unicorn.

YEAR	TEAM	LVL	AGE	PA	DRC+	VORP	BABIP	BRR	FRAA	WARP
2016	MIS	AA	24	342	78	3.7	.263	-1.5	C(75): 12.0, 1B(8): -0.7	1.1
2017	RNO	AAA	25	128	127	7.8	.330	-1.4	C(19): 0.9, 3B(14): 0.0	0.8
2018	ROC	AAA	26	307	110	16.0	.255	-1.4	C(39): 2.5, 3B(28): 0.6	1.3
2018	MIN	MLB	26	97	129	8.5	.341	0.4	C(16): 2.1, 3B(6): 0.0	1.0
2019	MIN	MLB	27	188	98	6.1	.270	-0.3	C 0, 3B -1	0.5

Willians Astudillo, continued

Batted Ball Distribution

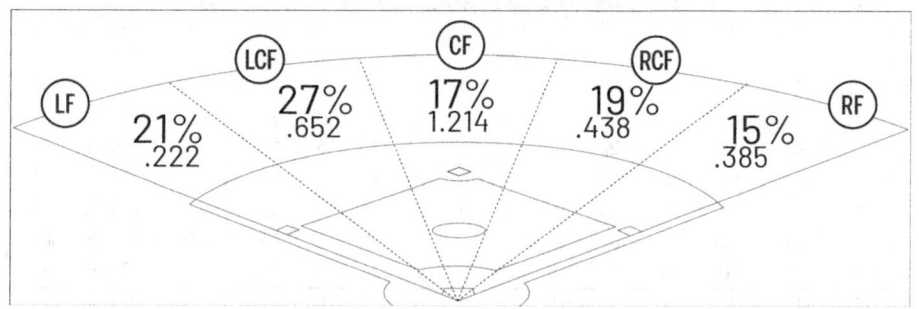

Strike Zone vs LHP   **Strike Zone vs RHP**

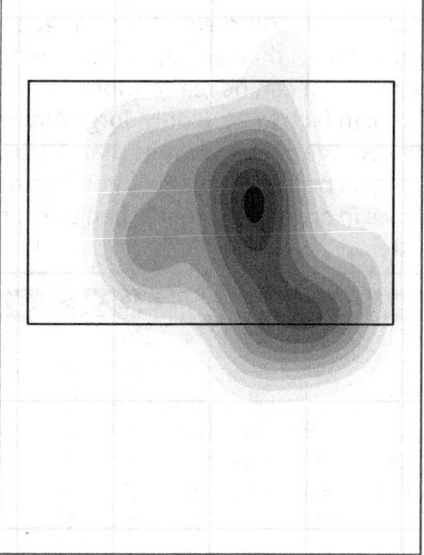

Tyler Austin 1B

Born: 09/06/91 Age: 27 Bats: R Throws: R
Height: 6'2" Weight: 220 Origin: Round 13, 2010 Draft (#415 overall)

YEAR	TEAM	LVL	AGE	PA	R	2B	3B	HR	RBI	BB	K	SB	CS	AVG/OBP/SLG
2016	TRN	AA	24	210	22	10	1	4	29	30	46	1	1	.260/.367/.395
2016	SWB	AAA	24	234	39	24	0	13	49	32	59	5	0	.323/.415/.637
2016	NYA	MLB	24	90	7	3	0	5	12	7	36	1	0	.241/.300/.458
2017	SWB	AAA	25	190	29	14	1	10	32	18	52	0	0	.275/.342/.544
2017	NYA	MLB	25	46	4	2	0	2	8	4	17	0	0	.225/.283/.425
2018	NYA	MLB	26	132	16	6	0	8	23	8	53	1	1	.223/.280/.471
2018	SWB	AAA	26	108	14	9	0	6	14	8	32	0	0	.253/.315/.525
2018	ROC	AAA	26	40	6	2	1	3	8	1	10	0	0	.263/.300/.605
2018	MIN	MLB	26	136	18	4	0	9	24	11	42	0	1	.236/.294/.488
2019	MIN	MLB	27	136	15	8	0	5	17	11	41	1	0	.228/.294/.415

Breakout: 12% Improve: 35% Collapse: 13% Attrition: 17% MLB: 62%
Comparables: Chris Carter, Tommy Medica, Juan Francisco

No batter in baseball leaves less doubt about what he's in the box to do. Austin had a greater differential in average exit velocity between his air balls and his ground balls than any other hitter with at least 100 batted balls. When he connects, it can be really impressive. Unfortunately, he doesn't connect all that often. In fact, in 2018 only Jorge Alfaro and Joey Gallo whiffed on a higher percentage of their swings than Austin. Not being an insanely tooled-up former Rangers prospect, Austin is going to need to make more contact or draw more walks in order to be more than a second-division first baseman/designated hitter.

YEAR	TEAM	LVL	AGE	PA	DRC+	VORP	BABIP	BRR	FRAA	WARP
2016	TRN	AA	24	210	119	7.2	.326	1.2	1B(37): 0.1, LF(7): -1.5	0.3
2016	SWB	AAA	24	234	189	26.9	.400	-0.2	1B(39): -3.5, RF(4): -0.3	1.9
2016	NYA	MLB	24	90	75	1.4	.357	0.3	1B(27): 1.9, RF(3): 0.0	0.0
2017	SWB	AAA	25	190	120	6.0	.336	-2.1	1B(23): 0.6, RF(4): 0.4	0.3
2017	NYA	MLB	25	46	79	0.3	.304	-0.5	1B(8): 0.0, RF(7): -0.5	-0.2
2018	NYA	MLB	26	132	95	0.0	.311	-0.1	1B(27): -1.3	0.0
2018	SWB	AAA	26	108	111	3.1	.311	0.0	1B(17): -0.6, RF(2): -0.5	0.0
2018	ROC	AAA	26	40	118	3.0	.280	-0.1	1B(7): -0.5	0.0
2018	MIN	MLB	26	136	100	3.9	.270	-0.3	1B(15): 0.1	0.2
2019	MIN	MLB	27	136	88	0.6	.299	-0.2	1B -1	0.0

Tyler Austin, continued

Batted Ball Distribution

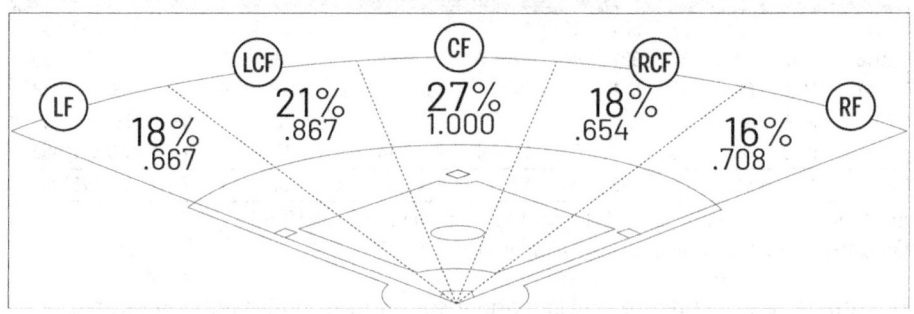

Strike Zone vs LHP   **Strike Zone vs RHP**

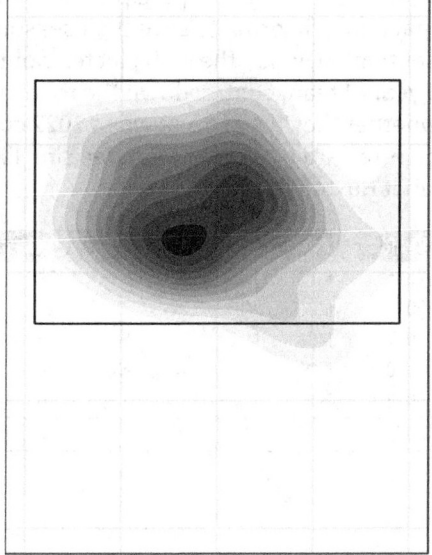

Byron Buxton CF

Born: 12/18/93 Age: 25 Bats: R Throws: R
Height: 6'2" Weight: 190 Origin: Round 1, 2012 Draft (#2 overall)

YEAR	TEAM	LVL	AGE	PA	R	2B	3B	HR	RBI	BB	K	SB	CS	AVG/OBP/SLG
2016	ROC	AAA	22	209	41	11	3	11	24	14	58	7	0	.305/.359/.568
2016	MIN	MLB	22	331	44	19	6	10	38	23	118	10	2	.225/.284/.430
2017	MIN	MLB	23	511	69	14	6	16	51	38	150	29	1	.253/.314/.413
2018	MIN	MLB	24	94	8	4	0	0	4	3	28	5	0	.156/.183/.200
2018	ROC	AAA	24	148	22	11	1	4	14	9	42	4	1	.272/.331/.456
2019	MIN	MLB	25	443	54	19	3	12	45	32	130	19	2	.234/.295/.386

Breakout: 12%   Improve: 56%   Collapse: 13%   Attrition: 18%   MLB: 95%
Comparables: Austin Jackson, Cameron Maybin, Adam Jones

Buxton has a truly unique skill set, and it sometimes makes him vulnerable to a unique set of problems. In 2018, those included a foot injury that (because his game relies so much on his speed, and because he even uses a toe tap to time the load phase of his swing) disproportionately wrecked his season; a crisis of offensive competence precipitated by the Twins' decision to rush him back from that injury, in order to save their season; and an unfair professional setback in September, when the club elected not to bring him back to the majors and lose a year of team control down the road, even as it remains an open question whether they'll want him when 2022 comes. Only an extraordinarily high-risk, high-reward player invites a decision like that one. At this point, that's exactly what Buxton is.

YEAR	TEAM	LVL	AGE	PA	DRC+	VORP	BABIP	BRR	FRAA	WARP
2016	ROC	AAA	22	209	140	23.7	.382	2.9	CF(47): -2.2	1.4
2016	MIN	MLB	22	331	70	10.3	.329	4.9	CF(92): 6.4	1.1
2017	MIN	MLB	23	511	86	17.0	.339	7.4	CF(137): 25.4	4.2
2018	MIN	MLB	24	94	57	-7.6	.226	0.3	CF(27): 1.4	0.0
2018	ROC	AAA	24	148	104	8.8	.367	1.4	CF(28): 9.0	1.3
2019	MIN	MLB	25	443	81	12.1	.307	3.3	CF 10	2.1

Byron Buxton, continued

Batted Ball Distribution

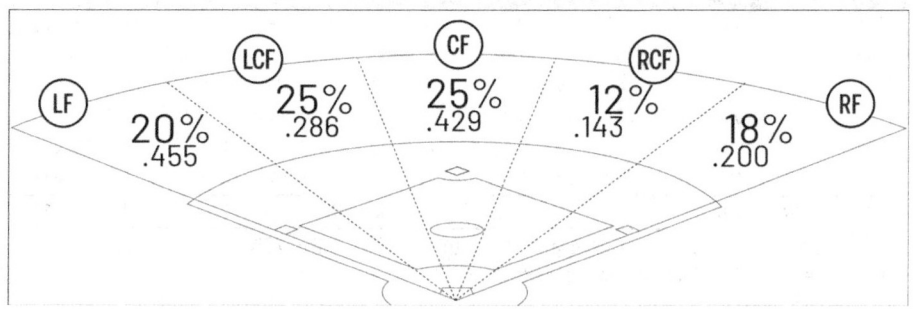

Strike Zone vs LHP   **Strike Zone vs RHP**

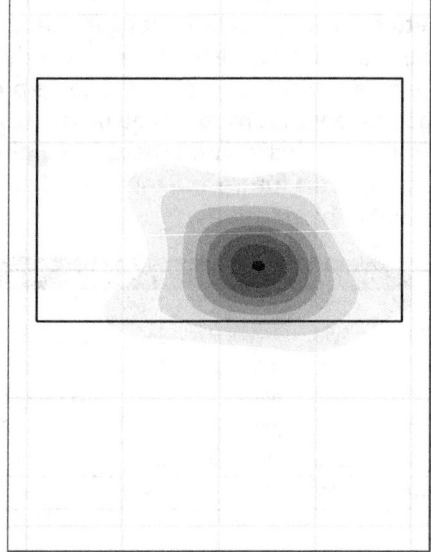

Jake Cave OF

Born: 12/04/92 Age: 26 Bats: L Throws: L
Height: 6'0" Weight: 200 Origin: Round 6, 2011 Draft (#209 overall)

YEAR	TEAM	LVL	AGE	PA	R	2B	3B	HR	RBI	BB	K	SB	CS	AVG/OBP/SLG
2016	TRN	AA	23	116	12	8	3	3	17	10	28	3	4	.288/.353/.510
2016	SWB	AAA	23	354	47	18	6	5	38	26	78	3	3	.261/.323/.401
2017	TRN	AA	24	140	19	13	2	5	18	10	33	1	0	.266/.317/.516
2017	SWB	AAA	24	297	47	13	3	15	38	18	82	1	3	.324/.367/.554
2018	ROC	AAA	25	250	26	9	1	6	28	26	55	4	2	.269/.352/.403
2018	MIN	MLB	25	309	54	16	2	13	45	18	102	2	1	.265/.313/.473
2019	MIN	MLB	26	256	29	11	1	9	30	17	74	2	1	.243/.297/.413

Breakout: 8% Improve: 46% Collapse: 11% Attrition: 28% MLB: 79%
Comparables: Scott Schebler, Ben Johnson, Brett Carroll

Everywhere, with Cave, the story is depth. No center fielder played deeper than he did in 2018. That's partially reflective of Minnesota's organizational philosophy about outfield positioning, but it served him well individually, too. Slightly stretched as a center fielder, given his merely average speed, Cave was better able to go back on long flies and to cut off hits to the gaps from his deeper starting point. He also hit some very deep home runs, demonstrating above-average power and generating some buzz based on sheer aesthetics. In the end, though, depth is probably all he is: his sky-high strikeout rate and failure to force big-league pitchers into the zone combine with the defensive questions to steer him toward a future as a fourth outfielder. Anything more, and Cave will likely be out of his depth.

YEAR	TEAM	LVL	AGE	PA	DRC+	VORP	BABIP	BRR	FRAA	WARP
2016	TRN	AA	23	116	121	7.7	.365	-0.6	LF(24): 2.1, CF(3): -0.1	0.5
2016	SWB	AAA	23	354	102	8.5	.329	-1.0	LF(43): -0.5, CF(28): 2.7	0.7
2017	TRN	AA	24	140	113	6.5	.319	-1.0	LF(17): 0.7, CF(7): -0.5	0.2
2017	SWB	AAA	24	297	145	25.5	.414	0.5	CF(30): -1.8, RF(25): 2.2	1.8
2018	ROC	AAA	25	250	114	13.0	.327	-0.1	RF(36): 5.4, CF(17): -0.6	1.3
2018	MIN	MLB	25	309	93	18.3	.363	3.1	CF(70): -7.5, RF(11): 0.3	0.3
2019	MIN	MLB	26	256	88	6.0	.315	-0.3	RF 0, CF -2	0.2

Jake Cave, continued

Batted Ball Distribution

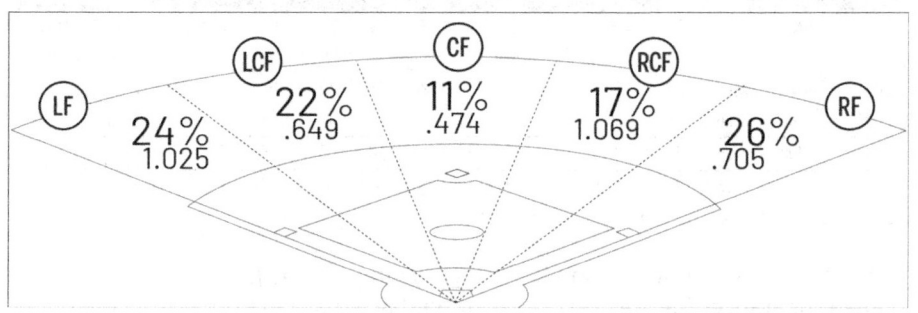

Strike Zone vs LHP   **Strike Zone vs RHP**

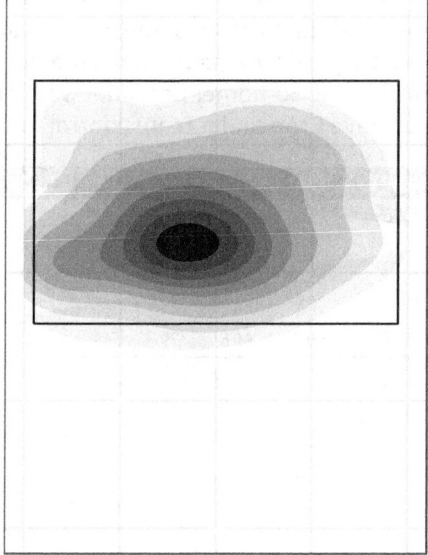

Minnesota Twins 2019

C.J. Cron 1B

Born: 01/05/90   Age: 29   Bats: R   Throws: R
Height: 6'4"   Weight: 235   Origin: Round 1, 2011 Draft (#17 overall)

YEAR	TEAM	LVL	AGE	PA	R	2B	3B	HR	RBI	BB	K	SB	CS	AVG/OBP/SLG
2016	ANA	MLB	26	445	51	25	2	16	69	24	75	2	3	.278/.325/.467
2017	SLC	AAA	27	96	11	6	0	4	23	7	15	1	0	.268/.344/.488
2017	ANA	MLB	27	373	39	14	1	16	56	22	96	3	2	.248/.305/.437
2018	TBA	MLB	28	560	68	28	1	30	74	37	145	1	2	.253/.323/.493
2019	MIN	MLB	29	532	72	27	1	21	64	40	120	3	2	.257/.327/.450

Breakout: 5%   Improve: 53%   Collapse: 21%   Attrition: 11%   MLB: 97%
Comparables: Adam Lind, Mitch Moreland, Mike Jacobs

Cron added a 30-homer season to his legacy while finally getting more than 500 plate appearances for the first time. Tampa Bay rewarded Cron by designating him for assignment and letting the Twins acquire his services for the cost of a waiver wire fee. Cron has legit power, but there's little else in the profile. Cron has sold out just a bit for the power, posting back-to-back seasons with at least 25 percent strikeouts. That number alone is not terrible, but the paltry walk rate does nothing to offset some ugly at-bats. Defensively, he's limited to first base and is typically passable there, making most routine plays. For a salary under $5 million, the 30-homer potential was certainly worth a shot for the Twins, who also have Cron under team control for 2020 via arbitration.

YEAR	TEAM	LVL	AGE	PA	DRC+	VORP	BABIP	BRR	FRAA	WARP
2016	ANA	MLB	26	445	111	12.4	.302	-2.0	1B(97): 2.6	1.2
2017	SLC	AAA	27	96	100	2.9	.273	0.0	1B(19): 0.9	0.1
2017	ANA	MLB	27	373	99	2.3	.296	-2.1	1B(98): 4.1	0.7
2018	TBA	MLB	28	560	118	18.0	.293	-3.5	1B(61): 2.6	1.9
2019	MIN	MLB	29	532	111	15.7	.301	-1.1	1B 4	2.1

C.J. Cron, continued

Batted Ball Distribution

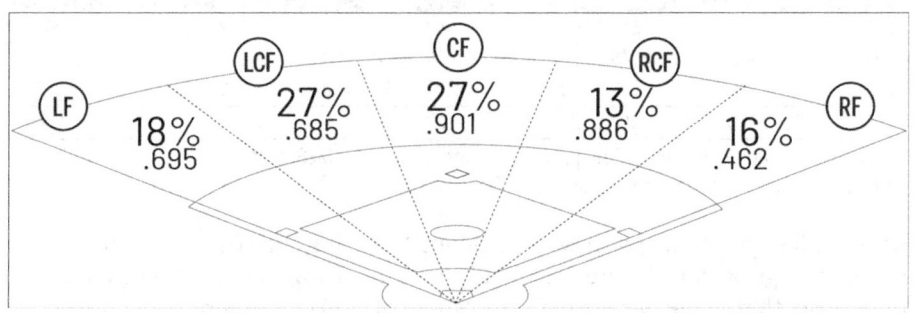

Strike Zone vs LHP   **Strike Zone vs RHP**

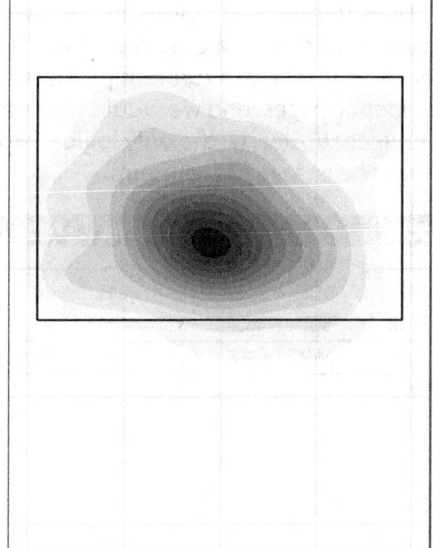

Nelson Cruz DH

Born: 07/01/80   Age: 38   Bats: R   Throws: R
Height: 6'2"   Weight: 230   Origin: International Free Agent, 1998

YEAR	TEAM	LVL	AGE	PA	R	2B	3B	HR	RBI	BB	K	SB	CS	AVG/OBP/SLG
2016	SEA	MLB	35	667	96	27	1	43	105	62	159	2	0	.287/.360/.555
2017	SEA	MLB	36	645	91	28	0	39	119	70	140	1	1	.288/.375/.549
2018	SEA	MLB	37	591	70	18	1	37	97	55	122	1	0	.256/.342/.509
2019	MIN	MLB	38	592	79	27	1	27	86	63	126	1	1	.270/.360/.483

Breakout: 0%   Improve: 15%   Collapse: 37%   Attrition: 13%   MLB: 81%
Comparables: Johnny Mize, Hank Aaron, David Ortiz

Ozymandias gets a bad wrap, so let's clear a few things up. The "vast and trunkless legs of stone" were Cruz's old shoes. Shoes wear out, so he got new ones. Also, that ruined visage with the "sneer of cold command" lying in the desert? That is collectively the group of people who mocked the Mariners for giving him a four-year contract, a period over which he hit 163 home runs, the most of any hitter in the game.

Does this mean that Nelson Cruz is not human, but rather some sort of immortal Home Run Golem striding through history and baseball, programmed by devious magic to torment pitchers for all of time? Of course not. These are academic pages, and we would never reduce ourselves to such pithy indulgence. Clearly, the only logical explanation for Cruz's late career explosion is that he is, in fact, a vampire.

YEAR	TEAM	LVL	AGE	PA	DRC+	VORP	BABIP	BRR	FRAA	WARP
2016	SEA	MLB	35	667	139	41.4	.320	-5.1	RF(48): -4.7	3.2
2017	SEA	MLB	36	645	143	40.4	.315	-1.8	RF(5): -0.1	4.2
2018	SEA	MLB	37	591	132	28.1	.264	-1.2	RF(4): 0.1	3.1
2019	MIN	MLB	38	592	131	30.0	.308	-1.1		3.3

Nelson Cruz, continued

Batted Ball Distribution

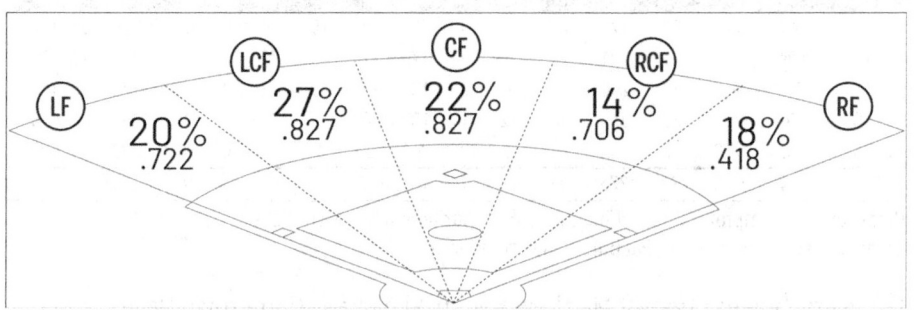

Strike Zone vs LHP **Strike Zone vs RHP**

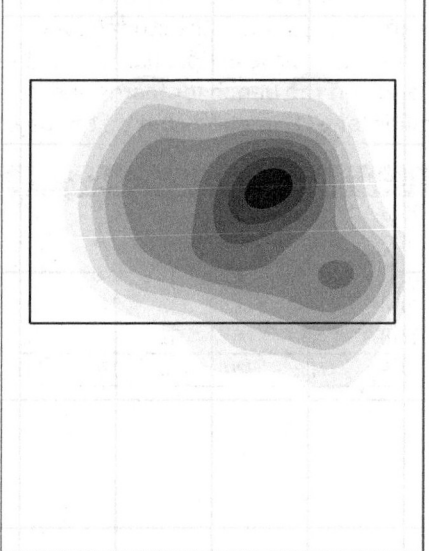

Minnesota Twins 2019

Lucas Duda 1B

Born: 02/03/86   Age: 33   Bats: L   Throws: R
Height: 6'4"   Weight: 255   Origin: Round 7, 2007 Draft (#243 overall)

YEAR	TEAM	LVL	AGE	PA	R	2B	3B	HR	RBI	BB	K	SB	CS	AVG/OBP/SLG
2016	NYN	MLB	30	172	20	7	0	7	23	15	36	0	0	.229/.302/.412
2017	NYN	MLB	31	291	30	21	0	17	37	37	73	0	0	.246/.347/.532
2017	TBA	MLB	31	200	20	7	0	13	27	23	62	0	0	.175/.285/.444
2018	KCA	MLB	32	345	34	12	1	13	48	24	95	1	0	.242/.310/.413
2018	ATL	MLB	32	22	1	2	0	1	2	4	7	0	0	.222/.364/.500
2019	MIN	MLB	33	376	42	18	1	13	49	32	94	1	0	.243/.321/.422

Breakout: 1%   Improve: 28%   Collapse: 15%   Attrition: 8%   MLB: 92%
Comparables: Andruw Jones, Pat Burrell, Adam LaRoche

For years, Braves organist Matthew Kaminski played "Camptown Races" when Duda came to the plate in Atlanta. Duda was once quoted as saying it stopped being funny after the 300th time he heard it. He got some relief in August when he was dealt to the Braves and could pick his own music at SunTrust Park. He also did his part in Atlanta by offering some power off the bench, something the team needed down the stretch for its playoff push. Duda's days of mashing full time at first base are probably over, but his left-handed power can come in handy off the bench for teams and keep his career going a while longer. Five miles long? Somebody bet on the bay.

YEAR	TEAM	LVL	AGE	PA	DRC+	VORP	BABIP	BRR	FRAA	WARP
2016	NYN	MLB	30	172	94	6.3	.250	0.7	1B(45): -3.4	-0.2
2017	NYN	MLB	31	291	112	13.1	.278	-3.4	1B(69): -1.7	0.3
2017	TBA	MLB	31	200	112	0.3	.173	0.1	1B(24): -0.2	0.6
2018	KCA	MLB	32	345	102	-0.1	.302	-2.4	1B(61): 2.4	0.5
2018	ATL	MLB	32	22	98	0.7	.300	-0.6	1B(2): -0.7	-0.1
2019	MIN	MLB	33	376	105	7.7	.300	-1.6	1B 0	0.8

Lucas Duda, continued

Batted Ball Distribution

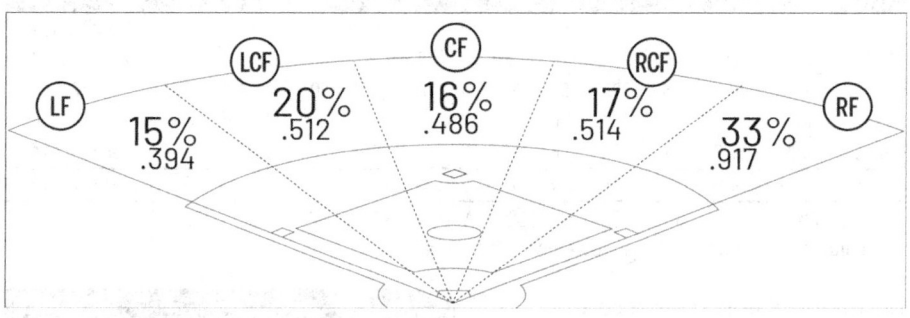

Strike Zone vs LHP   **Strike Zone vs RHP**

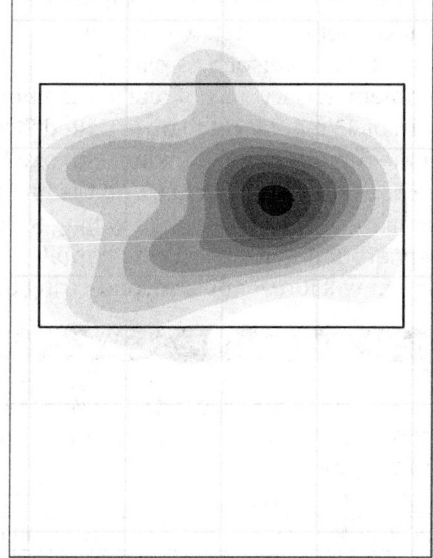

Mitch Garver C

Born: 01/15/91 Age: 28 Bats: R Throws: R
Height: 6'1" Weight: 220 Origin: Round 9, 2013 Draft (#260 overall)

YEAR	TEAM	LVL	AGE	PA	R	2B	3B	HR	RBI	BB	K	SB	CS	AVG/OBP/SLG
2016	CHT	AA	25	407	44	25	0	11	66	43	86	1	3	.257/.334/.419
2016	ROC	AAA	25	84	6	5	0	1	8	7	21	0	0	.329/.381/.434
2017	ROC	AAA	26	372	56	29	0	17	45	50	85	2	0	.291/.387/.541
2017	MIN	MLB	26	52	5	1	3	0	3	6	15	0	0	.196/.288/.348
2018	MIN	MLB	27	335	38	19	2	7	45	29	72	0	0	.268/.335/.414
2019	MIN	MLB	28	219	24	12	1	6	25	20	55	0	0	.254/.324/.416

Breakout: 6%   Improve: 35%   Collapse: 15%   Attrition: 34%   MLB: 74%
Comparables: Landon Powell, Ryan Lavarnway, Tommy Medica

His minor-league track record is tantalizing, but Garver raked there mostly as an overcooked prospect brought along too slowly. As a 27-year-old rookie in MLB, he was a slightly-below-average hitter, which is an acceptable level for a catcher. The problem is, Garver's not really a catcher. He's a dreadful pitch framer, ranking 27th of 33 regular catchers in Called Strikes Above Average. He's a poor stopper of the running game, ranking 58th of 67 qualifiers in pop time to second base. He does run like a catcher, and the bat isn't ever likely to play elsewhere, so he'll remain there as long as he's willing to take the abuse, but like the frat brother kept around only because he happily bears the brunt of everyone's jokes, Garver will forever be a second-string backstop in MLB.

YEAR	TEAM	P. COUNT	FRM RUNS	BLK RUNS	THRW RUNS	TOT RUNS
2017	MIN	832	-0.9	-0.1	0.0	-1.0
2017	ROC	8976	3.3	-0.9	0.4	2.5
2018	MIN	11726	-8.2	0.2	-0.4	-8.5
2019	MIN	7316	-3.4	-0.4	0.0	-3.7

YEAR	TEAM	LVL	AGE	PA	DRC+	VORP	BABIP	BRR	FRAA	WARP
2016	CHT	AA	25	407	114	18.4	.305	0.3	C(46): 7.3, 1B(14): -0.9	1.7
2016	ROC	AAA	25	84	126	7.0	.436	0.4	C(14): 0.1, 1B(2): -0.1	0.5
2017	ROC	AAA	26	372	160	40.4	.347	0.2	C(67): 3.6, LF(14): 0.9	3.9
2017	MIN	MLB	26	52	71	-1.0	.290	0.2	C(13): -1.1, 1B(3): 0.3	-0.1
2018	MIN	MLB	27	335	100	14.3	.330	-1.3	C(86): -8.5, 1B(5): -0.1	0.5
2019	MIN	MLB	28	219	103	10.1	.320	-0.4	C -5, 1B 0	0.4

Mitch Garver, continued

Batted Ball Distribution

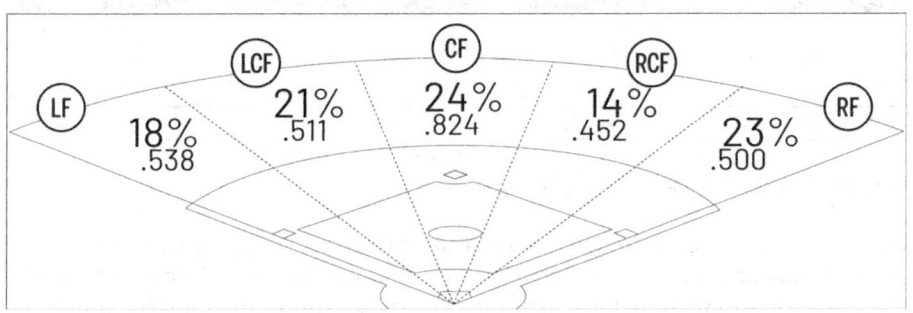

Strike Zone vs LHP   **Strike Zone vs RHP**

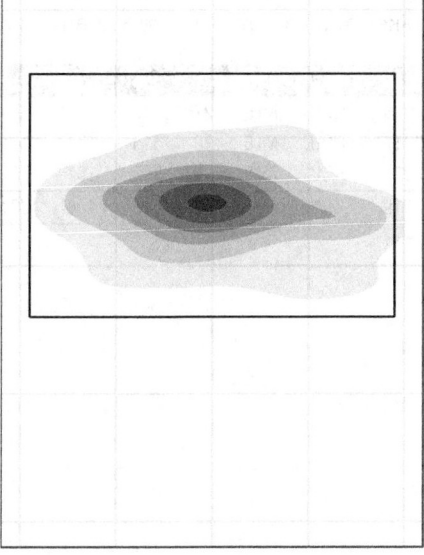

Marwin Gonzalez   UT

Born: 03/14/89   Age: 30   Bats: B   Throws: R
Height: 6'1"   Weight: 205   Origin: International Free Agent, 2005

YEAR	TEAM	LVL	AGE	PA	R	2B	3B	HR	RBI	BB	K	SB	CS	AVG/OBP/SLG
2016	HOU	MLB	27	518	55	26	3	13	51	22	118	12	6	.254/.293/.401
2017	HOU	MLB	28	515	67	34	0	23	90	49	99	8	3	.303/.377/.530
2018	HOU	MLB	29	552	61	25	3	16	68	53	126	2	3	.247/.324/.409
2019	MIN	MLB	30	528	62	27	2	16	64	46	112	6	4	.264/.336/.432

Breakout: 2%   Improve: 39%   Collapse: 16%   Attrition: 7%   MLB: 94%
Comparables: Hal McRae, Del Ennis, Eric Byrnes

Marwin Gonzalez continued in his super-utility role in 2018, playing every position except pitcher and catcher. He also dabbled in beer concessions on off days, served as part-time tax consultant for fellow teammates, and hand-crafted every World Series ring the Astros handed out at the beginning of the year. His offensive production paled in comparison to his stellar 2017 output, primarily because the 2018 version is who he really is. But especially in an era of three-man benches, the real Gonzalez, with his average bat and positional flexibility, makes him valuable to every team on the market.

YEAR	TEAM	LVL	AGE	PA	DRC+	VORP	BABIP	BRR	FRAA	WARP
2016	HOU	MLB	27	518	86	0.1	.311	-1.4	1B(92): 0.7, 3B(22): 0.6	0.2
2017	HOU	MLB	28	515	124	36.5	.343	-0.8	LF(47): -3.6, SS(38): -1.7	2.5
2018	HOU	MLB	29	552	101	22.8	.301	1.5	LF(73): 0.7, SS(39): -2.7	1.6
2019	MIN	MLB	30	528	106	20.8	.313	-0.7	2B -2, 3B 1	1.6

Marwin Gonzalez, continued

Batted Ball Distribution

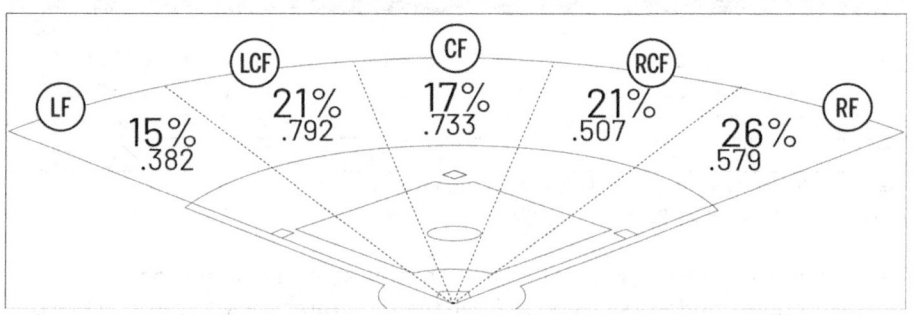

Strike Zone vs LHP   Strike Zone vs RHP

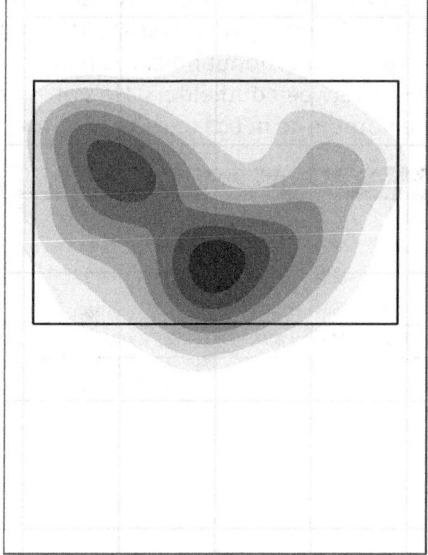

Max Kepler RF

Born: 02/10/93 Age: 26 Bats: L Throws: L
Height: 6'4" Weight: 205 Origin: International Free Agent, 2009

YEAR	TEAM	LVL	AGE	PA	R	2B	3B	HR	RBI	BB	K	SB	CS	AVG/OBP/SLG
2016	ROC	AAA	23	128	16	4	6	1	19	16	14	1	1	.282/.367/.455
2016	MIN	MLB	23	447	52	20	2	17	63	42	93	6	2	.235/.309/.424
2017	MIN	MLB	24	568	67	32	2	19	69	47	114	6	1	.243/.312/.425
2018	MIN	MLB	25	611	80	30	4	20	58	71	96	4	5	.224/.319/.408
2019	MIN	MLB	26	491	58	24	3	15	56	47	89	5	3	.244/.322/.416

Breakout: 4% Improve: 44% Collapse: 11% Attrition: 13% MLB: 96%
Comparables: Andre Ethier, Ryan Sweeney, Blake DeWitt

On the surface, perhaps, Kepler had a frustrating season of non-progress. Dig deeper, though, and the signs point in all the right directions. In the absence of Byron Buxton, Kepler proved to be a perfectly cromulent center fielder. He swung significantly more often at pitches within the strike zone, and significantly less at those outside it. He made hard contact more frequently, but also swung and missed less often within the strike zone. For the second straight season, he embiggened his launch angle. He just hit too many balls that fell into the proverbial donut hole: too hard to become bloop singles, too high to get down between outfielders. He's one more set of small adjustments from hitting the homers he needs to round out his profile.

YEAR	TEAM	LVL	AGE	PA	DRC+	VORP	BABIP	BRR	FRAA	WARP
2016	ROC	AAA	23	128	116	7.5	.309	0.7	RF(26): 1.9, CF(6): 0.4	0.7
2016	MIN	MLB	23	447	101	6.3	.261	0.9	RF(108): 3.6, CF(4): -0.1	1.4
2017	MIN	MLB	24	568	90	1.1	.276	-2.2	RF(138): 5.1, CF(13): 0.3	0.9
2018	MIN	MLB	25	611	102	16.5	.236	2.7	RF(117): 10.2, CF(55): -1.3	2.9
2019	MIN	MLB	26	491	99	14.8	.274	-0.4	RF 4, CF 0	1.7

Max Kepler, continued

Batted Ball Distribution

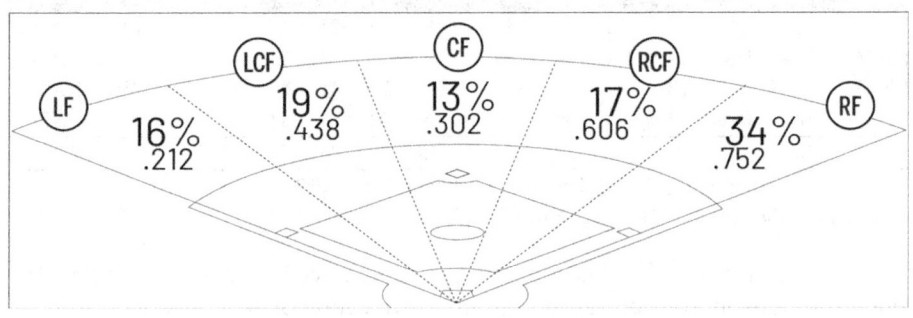

Strike Zone vs LHP **Strike Zone vs RHP**

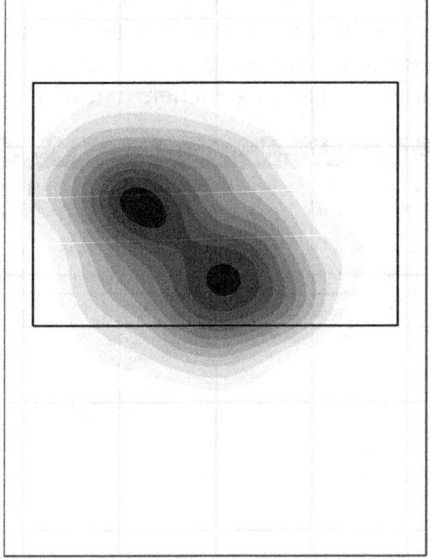

Jorge Polanco SS

Born: 07/05/93   Age: 25   Bats: B   Throws: R
Height: 5'11"   Weight: 200   Origin: International Free Agent, 2009

YEAR	TEAM	LVL	AGE	PA	R	2B	3B	HR	RBI	BB	K	SB	CS	AVG/OBP/SLG
2016	ROC	AAA	22	325	32	14	6	9	39	27	51	5	4	.276/.335/.457
2016	MIN	MLB	22	270	24	15	4	4	27	17	46	4	3	.282/.332/.424
2017	MIN	MLB	23	544	60	30	3	13	74	41	78	13	5	.256/.313/.410
2018	MIN	MLB	24	333	38	18	3	6	42	25	62	7	7	.288/.345/.427
2019	MIN	MLB	25	535	60	27	4	13	59	40	90	11	7	.260/.320/.413

Breakout: 11%   Improve: 69%   Collapse: 2%   Attrition: 23%   MLB: 97%
Comparables: Didi Gregorius, Jurickson Profar, Russ Adams

Thanks to a rush-job of a minor-league career, Polanco has taken a long time to find his footing in the majors. The self-inflicted wound of an 80-game suspension for performance-enhancing drugs only exacerbated that problem last year. He continues to make progress in terms of controlling the zone; he attacks strikes and doesn't chase junk. There's still no sign that he'll develop real over-the-fence power, though. He's a fine athlete, but neither a good baserunner nor a viable shortstop. Polanco's chances to emerge as more than a second-division second baseman hinge on his ability to continue hitting line drives and forcing pitchers to throw strikes.

YEAR	TEAM	LVL	AGE	PA	DRC+	VORP	BABIP	BRR	FRAA	WARP
2016	ROC	AAA	22	325	127	17.5	.304	0.3	2B(64): 5.7, 3B(2): 0.2	2.0
2016	MIN	MLB	22	270	96	9.3	.328	-0.7	SS(47): -1.9, 3B(9): -0.8	0.6
2017	MIN	MLB	23	544	90	17.1	.278	0.8	SS(130): -9.2	0.9
2018	MIN	MLB	24	333	97	12.9	.345	-3.0	SS(76): -9.7	0.1
2019	MIN	MLB	25	535	94	16.8	.291	-0.4	SS -8	0.8

Jorge Polanco, continued

Batted Ball Distribution

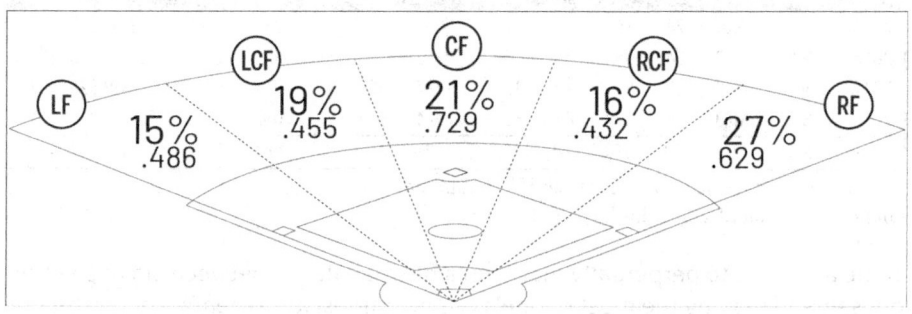

Strike Zone vs LHP   **Strike Zone vs RHP**

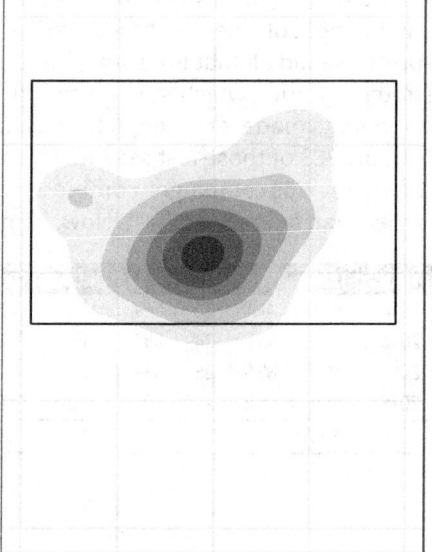

Eddie Rosario LF

Born: 09/28/91　Age: 27　Bats: L　Throws: R
Height: 6'1"　Weight: 180　Origin: Round 4, 2010 Draft (#135 overall)

YEAR	TEAM	LVL	AGE	PA	R	2B	3B	HR	RBI	BB	K	SB	CS	AVG/OBP/SLG
2016	ROC	AAA	24	169	26	14	0	7	25	7	25	5	3	.319/.343/.538
2016	MIN	MLB	24	354	52	17	2	10	32	12	91	5	2	.269/.295/.421
2017	MIN	MLB	25	589	79	33	2	27	78	35	106	9	8	.290/.328/.507
2018	MIN	MLB	26	592	87	31	2	24	77	30	104	8	2	.288/.323/.479
2019	MIN	MLB	27	580	79	32	3	21	69	36	110	9	5	.278/.325/.466

Breakout: 7%　Improve: 51%　Collapse: 12%　Attrition: 10%　MLB: 96%
Comparables: Marcell Ozuna, Joe Rudi, Bibb Falk

To be a hitter is to perpetually maintain a fragile balance between staying within oneself and making the most of one's opportunities. It's a mental challenge and a physical one, and it's complicated by the opposition's constant effort to force an adjustment that might tip one out of balance. For a solid year, however, Rosario found that balance. From July 14, 2017 through July 15, 2018, he batted .303/.343/.546, with 44 doubles and 36 homers in 695 plate appearances. He did it in the heat of a pennant race, and in the cold of a bitter and disappointing spring. He did all that for a year, but on either side of that window were long stretches during which Rosario couldn't keep up with the adjustments opponents made, or wherein he was flummoxed by things like defensive shifts. (He saw 263 of those last season, more by a wide margin than he had seen in his three previous campaigns combined.) He's learned to use his aggressiveness, rather than being used by it. Now, he needs to learn to do it all the time.

YEAR	TEAM	LVL	AGE	PA	DRC+	VORP	BABIP	BRR	FRAA	WARP
2016	ROC	AAA	24	169	154	13.3	.338	1.1	CF(29): 2.6, RF(9): 3.0	2.0
2016	MIN	MLB	24	354	83	9.0	.338	4.4	LF(57): 0.7, CF(37): -1.9	0.6
2017	MIN	MLB	25	589	107	18.1	.312	-1.6	LF(138): -2.7, RF(16): 0.2	1.6
2018	MIN	MLB	26	592	112	29.9	.316	6.8	LF(125): 5.9, RF(5): -0.2	3.6
2019	MIN	MLB	27	580	105	24.1	.311	-0.4	LF -1	1.9

Eddie Rosario, continued

Batted Ball Distribution

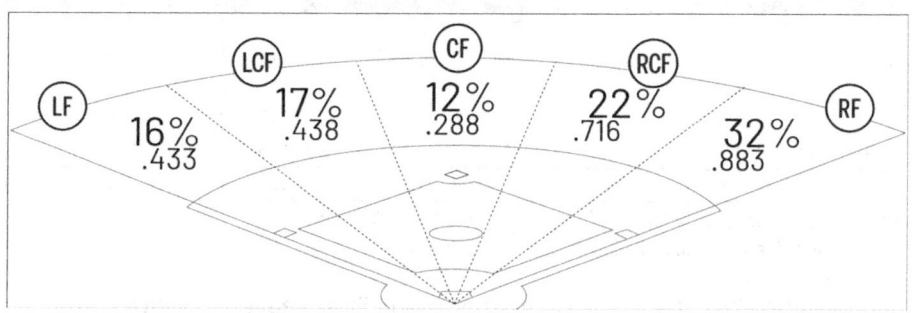

Strike Zone vs LHP **Strike Zone vs RHP**

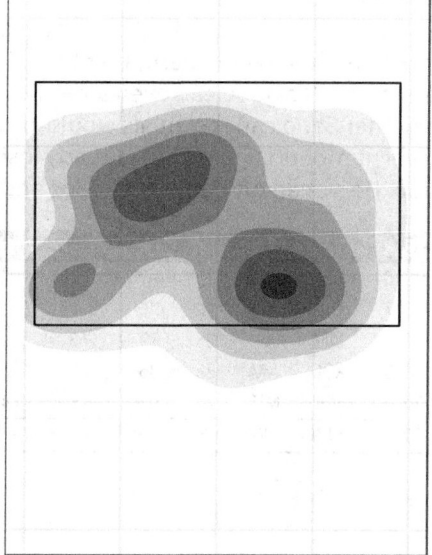

Twins Player Analysis - 43

Minnesota Twins 2019

Miguel Sano 3B
Born: 05/11/93   Age: 26   Bats: R   Throws: R
Height: 6'4"   Weight: 260   Origin: International Free Agent, 2009

YEAR	TEAM	LVL	AGE	PA	R	2B	3B	HR	RBI	BB	K	SB	CS	AVG/OBP/SLG
2016	MIN	MLB	23	495	57	22	1	25	66	54	178	1	0	.236/.319/.462
2017	MIN	MLB	24	483	75	15	2	28	77	54	173	0	0	.264/.352/.507
2018	FTM	A+	25	77	11	2	0	2	12	13	21	0	0	.328/.442/.453
2018	ROC	AAA	25	36	2	1	0	2	5	6	8	0	0	.267/.389/.500
2018	MIN	MLB	25	299	32	14	0	13	41	31	115	0	0	.199/.281/.398
2019	MIN	MLB	26	520	70	22	1	21	62	58	174	1	0	.233/.323/.424

Breakout: 3%   Improve: 49%   Collapse: 12%   Attrition: 9%   MLB: 98%
Comparables: Mark Reynolds, Pedro Alvarez, Mike Schmidt

Sano handled his June demotion to the Florida State League as well as could be hoped under the circumstances. It's the only thing he's done right since late summer 2017. Plagued by very real questions of makeup and off-field comportment, he was unable even to answer the pressing on-field questions about his future in 2018. It's not clear whether his Brobdingnagian body will allow him to remain a third baseman, especially as injury issues persist (indeed, as symbolized by the permanent titanium rod in his shin, they seem to be going nowhere). It's not clear, even after over 1,600 trips to the plate in the majors, whether Sano can reel in his would-be historic strikeout rate, and the process-level numbers suggest he's already losing some of his would-have-been historic pop. He's at an off-field crossroads and an on-field nadir.

YEAR	TEAM	LVL	AGE	PA	DRC+	VORP	BABIP	BRR	FRAA	WARP
2016	MIN	MLB	23	495	102	13.6	.329	2.0	3B(42): 6.5, RF(38): -1.9	2.0
2017	MIN	MLB	24	483	119	22.5	.375	-2.0	3B(82): -5.9, 1B(9): 1.2	1.9
2018	FTM	A+	25	77	163	7.8	.463	0.2	3B(10): 0.4	0.6
2018	ROC	AAA	25	36	129	2.7	.300	0.2	3B(4): 1.5, 1B(1): 0.0	0.3
2018	MIN	MLB	25	299	83	-0.4	.286	-1.0	3B(56): 0.1, 1B(11): 0.1	0.2
2019	MIN	MLB	26	520	106	16.1	.324	-1.0	3B 0, 1B 1	1.7

Miguel Sano, continued

Batted Ball Distribution

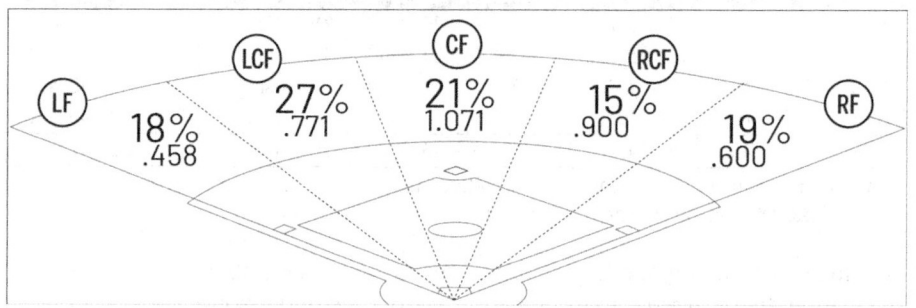

Strike Zone vs LHP　　　**Strike Zone vs RHP**

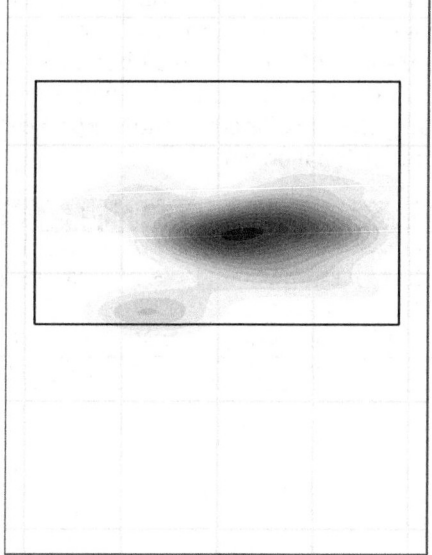

Jonathan Schoop 2B

Born: 10/16/91 Age: 27 Bats: R Throws: R
Height: 6'1" Weight: 225 Origin: International Free Agent, 2008

YEAR	TEAM	LVL	AGE	PA	R	2B	3B	HR	RBI	BB	K	SB	CS	AVG/OBP/SLG
2016	BAL	MLB	24	647	82	38	1	25	82	21	137	1	2	.267/.298/.454
2017	BAL	MLB	25	675	92	35	0	32	105	35	142	1	0	.293/.338/.503
2018	BAL	MLB	26	367	45	18	1	17	40	12	74	0	1	.244/.273/.447
2018	MIL	MLB	26	134	16	4	0	4	21	7	41	1	0	.202/.246/.331
2019	MIN	MLB	27	437	49	22	1	16	57	25	89	1	1	.266/.317/.445

Breakout: 6% Improve: 52% Collapse: 7% Attrition: 2% MLB: 95%
Comparables: Jeff Kent, Bret Boone, Jim Morrison

Outside of a smoking hot July, Schoop batted .198/.242/.340 in 2018, crashing back down to earth after an All-Star campaign. He could not crack a .400 slugging percentage in any of those other spring or summer months. This marked a stunning reversal from an excellent 32-homer campaign in 2017. Schoop's power promise fully materialized that year, with the notable new-school and old-school trophies of a .500 slugging percentage and 100 RBI. The toughest aspect of Schoop's decline is explaining the prime age reversion; but entering 2019 as an age-27 batter, Schoop sees his strikeouts creeping up, walks dwindling away and ground balls increasing. Not every prime-age player has large margins for error, and Schoop demonstrates the hazards of one-dimensional power.

YEAR	TEAM	LVL	AGE	PA	DRC+	VORP	BABIP	BRR	FRAA	WARP
2016	BAL	MLB	24	647	96	12.3	.305	1.5	2B(162): -2.4	1.5
2017	BAL	MLB	25	675	115	37.6	.330	4.2	2B(159): 8.2, SS(5): 0.8	4.7
2018	BAL	MLB	26	367	83	5.6	.262	-0.6	2B(85): 7.9, SS(2): 0.0	1.1
2018	MIL	MLB	26	134	83	-1.1	.259	1.0	2B(31): 1.4, SS(15): 1.1	0.5
2019	MIN	MLB	27	437	106	20.5	.303	-0.9	2B 2	2.0

Jonathan Schoop, continued

Batted Ball Distribution

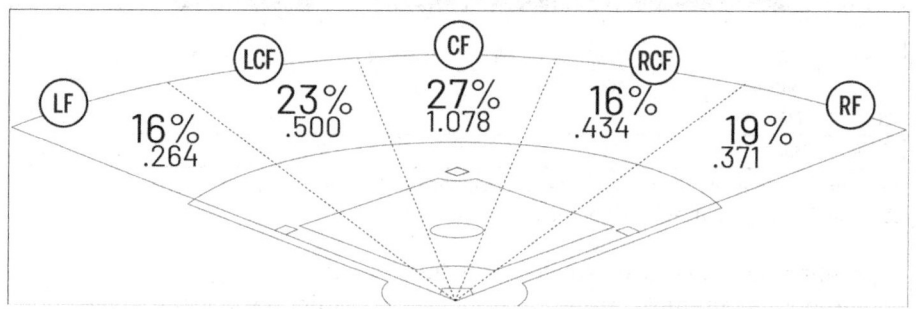

Strike Zone vs LHP   **Strike Zone vs RHP**

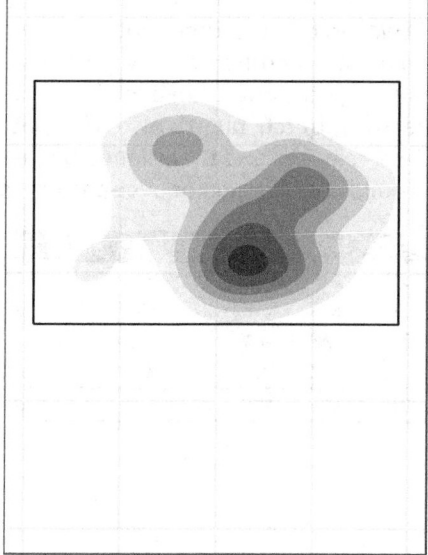

Twins Player Analysis - 47

Ronald Torreyes INF
Born: 09/02/92   Age: 26   Bats: R   Throws: R
Height: 5'8"   Weight: 151   Origin: International Free Agent, 2010

YEAR	TEAM	LVL	AGE	PA	R	2B	3B	HR	RBI	BB	K	SB	CS	AVG/OBP/SLG
2016	NYA	MLB	23	168	20	7	4	1	12	10	20	2	1	.258/.305/.374
2017	NYA	MLB	24	336	35	15	1	3	36	11	43	2	0	.292/.314/.375
2018	SWB	AAA	25	106	9	3	0	0	8	7	11	0	0	.247/.302/.278
2018	NYA	MLB	25	102	9	7	1	0	7	2	16	0	0	.280/.294/.370
2019	MIN	MLB	26	29	3	1	0	0	2	2	4	0	0	.222/.276/.259

Breakout: 8%   Improve: 55%   Collapse: 6%   Attrition: 28%   MLB: 93%
Comparables: Steve Lombardozzi, Donovan Solano, Darwin Barney

Even when the Yankees are stocked with juggernaut after juggernaut, sometimes fan attention zeroes in on players with minimal statistical value but maximal "team" value, however that can be weighed. Luis Sojo comes to mind, though he did have 2000 World Series bonafides to hold up. Torreyes doesn't have those, though he possesses all of the Sojoian qualities to endear himself to fans — a dynamic and fun personality, solid defense and a high batting average. He was so highly touted that fans grumbled when he was sent down after the infield roster crunch, and some probably would even go so far that their second half slog was attributable to his intangibles missing from the team. That logic is clearly a stretch, but it's also true that every foot needs a Big Toe. Traded to the Cubs, released and then signed by the Twins, Torreyes will have the opportunity to build a new legion of over-enthusiastic fans at Target Field.

YEAR	TEAM	LVL	AGE	PA	DRC+	VORP	BABIP	BRR	FRAA	WARP
2016	NYA	MLB	23	168	86	4.6	.289	0.9	3B(34): 4.3, SS(15): -1.2	0.6
2017	NYA	MLB	24	336	84	5.2	.326	1.3	2B(54): 0.8, SS(36): 0.5	1.0
2018	SWB	AAA	25	106	85	-0.7	.276	-0.4	2B(11): -1.1, 3B(6): -0.4	-0.1
2018	NYA	MLB	25	102	82	-0.5	.333	-0.4	2B(20): -0.4, 3B(11): 0.6	0.2
2019	MIN	MLB	26	29	87	0.4	.291	0.0	3B 1	0.1

Ronald Torreyes, continued

Batted Ball Distribution

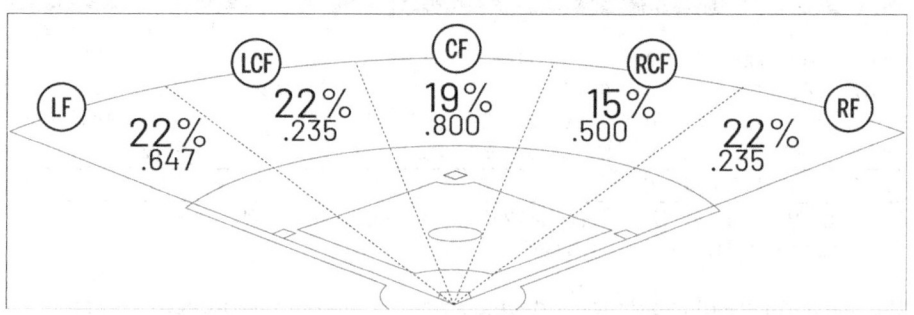

Strike Zone vs LHP   **Strike Zone vs RHP**

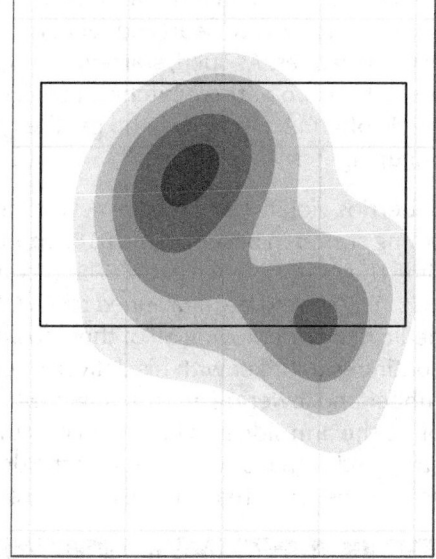

Jose Berrios   RHP

Born: 05/27/94   Age: 25   Bats: R   Throws: R
Height: 6'0"   Weight: 185   Origin: Round 1, 2012 Draft (#32 overall)

YEAR	TEAM	LVL	AGE	W	L	SV	G	GS	IP	H	HR	BB/9	K/9	K	GB%	BABIP
2016	ROC	AAA	22	10	5	0	17	17	111^1	74	8	2.9	10.1	125	45%	.254
2016	MIN	MLB	22	3	7	0	14	14	58^1	74	12	5.4	7.6	49	39%	.344
2017	ROC	AAA	23	3	0	0	6	6	39^2	24	2	1.8	8.8	39	40%	.214
2017	MIN	MLB	23	14	8	0	26	25	145^2	131	15	3.0	8.6	139	41%	.289
2018	MIN	MLB	24	12	11	0	32	32	192^1	159	25	2.9	9.5	202	43%	.270
2019	MIN	MLB	25	12	9	0	30	30	180	158	21	3.3	9.3	187	42%	.289

Breakout: 29%   Improve: 57%   Collapse: 22%   Attrition: 16%   MLB: 98%
Comparables: Daniel Hudson, Michael Pineda, Clay Buchholz

We live in an era of rapid player development, simplified approaches and a constantly changing set of quick-fix proposals to heal what ails any young player failing to live up to their billing. We also live in *the* era of the five-inning ace. The third time through the order is the danger zone for most starters, and rather than try to fix that in any way, teams have accepted it as the natural state of the game. Relievers are nearly equal partners with starters in the daily endeavor of winning games. As such, starters are expected to develop as rapidly as relievers do: to find two or three pitches that work for them, focus on the most dominant single offering in that mix and get the hell out of there before the opposing lineup figures them out.

Berrios violates all of those new norms. He's as true a throwback as any young starter in baseball. In 2018, opposing batters posted a .667 OPS the first time they saw him in a game. The second time through, that ticked up to only .679. The third time, it *dropped* to .637. Berrios uses four pitches, and is fairly dedicated to deploying all of them to advantage during each contest. He continues to tinker with his delivery, getting way to the third-base side of the rubber and lowering his arm angle, which has really allowed his sinker to take off to the arm side and has given his curveball a slider shape. He wore down and struggled with his control during the dog days in 2018, but in his third full season, he looks ready to be a consistent and often dominant workhorse.

YEAR	TEAM	LVL	AGE	WHIP	ERA	DRA	WARP	MPH	FB%	WHF	CSP
2016	ROC	AAA	22	0.99	2.51	2.67	3.4				
2016	MIN	MLB	22	1.87	8.02	7.42	-1.4	95.9	64	9	43.8
2017	ROC	AAA	23	0.81	1.13	3.49	1.0				
2017	MIN	MLB	23	1.23	3.89	4.29	2.1	95.9	61.5	10.5	46.4
2018	MIN	MLB	24	1.14	3.84	4.25	2.4	95.2	60.4	12.3	46.7
2019	MIN	MLB	25	1.24	3.69	4.05	2.9	95.2	62.7	11.6	47

Jose Berrios, continued

Pitch Shape vs LHH

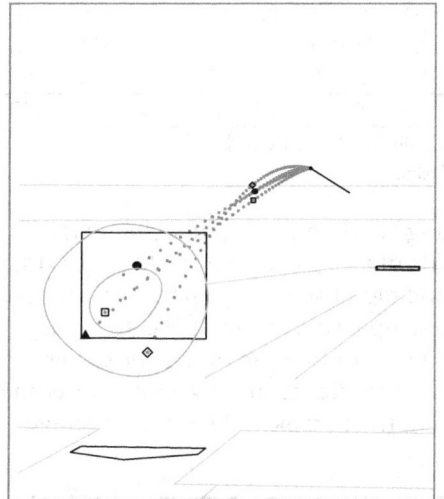

Pitch Shape vs RHH

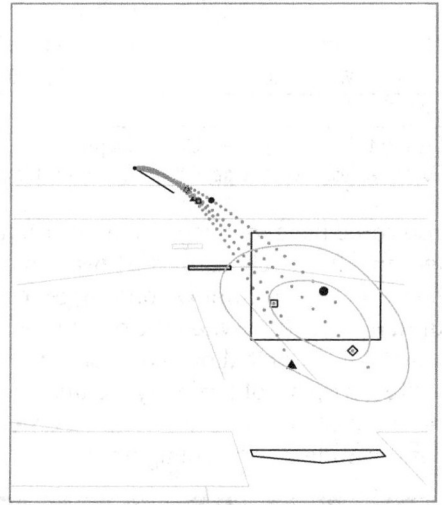

Type	Frequency	Velocity	H Movement	V Movement
● Fastball	34.6%	93.8 [104]	-8.6 [91]	-14.3 [105]
☐ Sinker	25.8%	93.2 [104]	-14.1 [87]	-19.1 [104]
+ Cutter				
▲ Changeup	9.1%	84.1 [95]	-12.4 [94]	-31.2 [89]
✕ Splitter				
▽ Slider				
◇ Curveball	30.4%	82 [113]	14 [126]	-38.1 [122]
⊕ Slow Curveball				
✱ Knuckleball				
▼ Screwball				

Tim Collins LHP

Born: 08/21/89 Age: 29 Bats: L Throws: L
Height: 5'7" Weight: 168 Origin: Undrafted Free Agent, 2007

YEAR	TEAM	LVL	AGE	W	L	SV	G	GS	IP	H	HR	BB/9	K/9	K	GB%	BABIP
2017	HAR	AA	27	1	1	0	10	0	8²	12	2	10.4	8.3	8	48%	.370
2018	SYR	AAA	28	2	4	0	30	0	32	26	0	4.2	9.6	34	55%	.313
2018	WAS	MLB	28	0	0	0	38	0	22²	23	5	4.8	8.3	21	41%	.295
2019	MIN	MLB	29	2	1	0	36	0	38²	37	6	5.5	9.0	38	47%	.297

Breakout: 11%   Improve: 20%   Collapse: 27%   Attrition: 26%   MLB: 50%
Comparables: Lucas Luetge, Preston Claiborne, Clay Zavada

You could have forgiven Collins for thinking his all-important left elbow was a lemon. After pitching for the Royals in parts of every season from 2011 to 2014, he endured two Tommy John surgeries and didn't see action in the majors again until May of 2018. When the diminutive southpaw did return, it was sweet as sugar — he didn't allow a run for more than a month. Even though he didn't quite gin up his old velocity, Collins added some fizz to the mix with a cutter that he threw almost 18 percent of the time, and then drank in the league-average results under the bright lights.

YEAR	TEAM	LVL	AGE	WHIP	ERA	DRA	WARP	MPH	FB%	WHF	CSP
2017	HAR	AA	27	2.54	14.54	4.74	0.0				
2018	SYR	AAA	28	1.28	3.94	3.65	0.5				
2018	WAS	MLB	28	1.54	4.37	4.37	0.1	93.4	53.4	12.4	44.7
2019	MIN	MLB	29	1.58	5.14	5.40	-0.1	92.7	53.4	12.4	44.7

Tim Collins, continued

Pitch Shape vs LHH

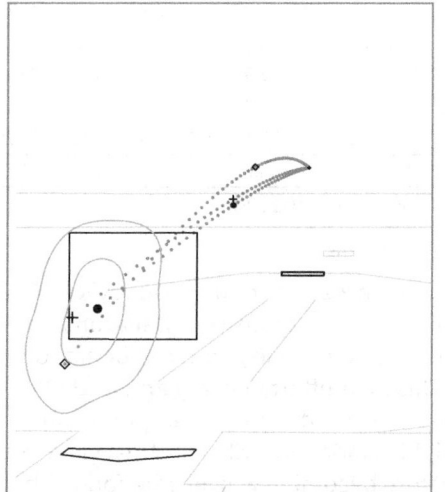

Pitch Shape vs RHH

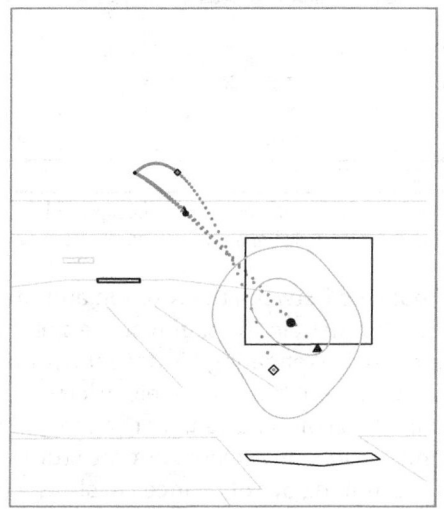

Type	Frequency	Velocity	H Movement	V Movement
● Fastball	53.4%	92.7 [101]	3.3 [115]	-12.1 [112]
☐ Sinker				
+ Cutter	17.8%	89.1 [102]	-4 [112]	-21.4 [109]
▲ Changeup	11.6%	84.3 [96]	7.2 [122]	-18.3 [127]
✕ Splitter				
▽ Slider				
◇ Curveball	17.3%	75.1 [87]	-8.6 [103]	-59.8 [74]
⊕ Slow Curveball				
✱ Knuckleball				
▼ Screwball				

Minnesota Twins 2019

Tyler Duffey   RHP
Born: 12/27/90   Age: 28   Bats: R   Throws: R
Height: 6'3"   Weight: 220   Origin: Round 5, 2012 Draft (#160 overall)

YEAR	TEAM	LVL	AGE	W	L	SV	G	GS	IP	H	HR	BB/9	K/9	K	GB%	BABIP
2016	ROC	AAA	25	1	1	0	5	5	30^2	24	4	3.5	7.3	25	35%	.238
2016	MIN	MLB	25	9	12	0	26	26	133	167	25	2.2	7.7	114	49%	.339
2017	MIN	MLB	26	2	3	1	56	0	71	79	9	2.3	8.5	67	50%	.326
2018	ROC	AAA	27	4	4	3	31	0	59	48	5	3.1	9.6	63	45%	.277
2018	MIN	MLB	27	2	2	0	19	1	25	26	6	1.4	6.8	19	35%	.260
2019	MIN	MLB	28	2	2	0	33	0	34	32	4	3.3	8.6	33	44%	.293

Breakout: 23%   Improve: 46%   Collapse: 21%   Attrition: 29%   MLB: 90%
Comparables: Billy Traber, Liam Hendriks, Randy Wells

Bouncing between the rotation and the bullpen wasn't good for Duffey's development in the slightest. He spent his formative professional seasons focused on repeating his delivery, arm speed and release point, but doing so stole some of the natural electricity from his high-effort delivery and fastball-curveball combination. Starting meant working hard to remain unpredictable and emotionally steady, but the sturdy right-hander is a wild southpaw at heart. He's running out of chances to show it before becoming waiver wire fodder, but somewhere within Duffey's profile lurks a setup man whose intensity and sheer stuff make life difficult for opposing hitters.

YEAR	TEAM	LVL	AGE	WHIP	ERA	DRA	WARP	MPH	FB%	WHF	CSP
2016	ROC	AAA	25	1.17	2.93	5.54	-0.1				
2016	MIN	MLB	25	1.50	6.43	6.01	-1.0	93.2	54.5	9.3	46.2
2017	MIN	MLB	26	1.37	4.94	3.65	1.2	93.8	59.4	11.8	48
2018	ROC	AAA	27	1.15	2.90	4.48	0.4				
2018	MIN	MLB	27	1.20	7.20	5.41	-0.1	95.2	61.2	11.3	48.5
2019	MIN	MLB	28	1.29	3.78	4.17	0.4	93.2	57.5	10.5	48

Tyler Duffey, continued

Pitch Shape vs LHH

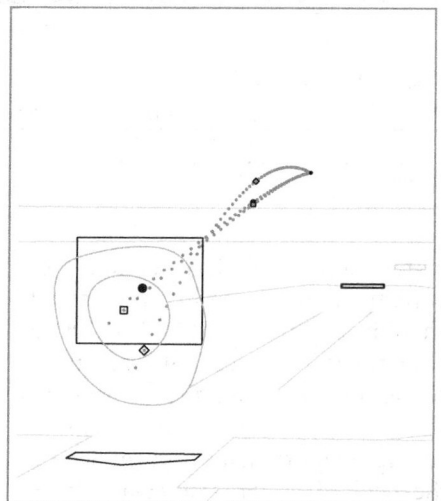

Pitch Shape vs RHH

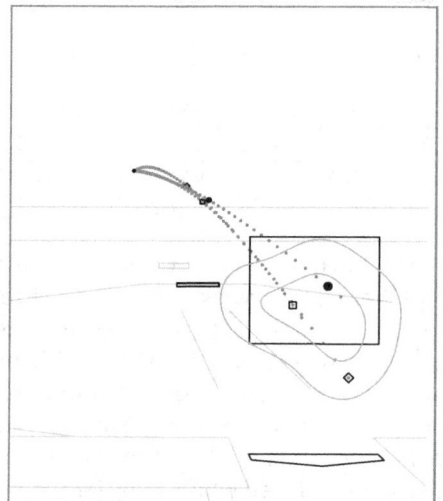

Type	Frequency	Velocity	H Movement	V Movement
● Fastball	36.5%	93.4 [103]	-4.4 [110]	-14.7 [103]
□ Sinker	24.7%	93.2 [104]	-12 [105]	-21.1 [97]
+ Cutter				
▲ Changeup	5.0%	84.9 [98]	-12.2 [95]	-27.9 [98]
× Splitter				
▽ Slider				
◇ Curveball	33.8%	80.7 [108]	8.8 [104]	-49.8 [96]
⊕ Slow Curveball				
✳ Knuckleball				
▼ Screwball				

Kyle Gibson RHP

Born: 10/23/87 Age: 31 Bats: R Throws: R
Height: 6'6" Weight: 215 Origin: Round 1, 2009 Draft (#22 overall)

YEAR	TEAM	LVL	AGE	W	L	SV	G	GS	IP	H	HR	BB/9	K/9	K	GB%	BABIP
2016	MIN	MLB	28	6	11	0	25	25	147^1	175	20	3.4	6.4	104	50%	.330
2017	ROC	AAA	29	1	2	0	3	3	17^1	13	1	2.6	11.9	23	60%	.308
2017	MIN	MLB	29	12	10	0	29	29	158	182	24	3.4	6.9	121	52%	.328
2018	MIN	MLB	30	10	13	0	32	32	196^2	177	23	3.6	8.2	179	51%	.285
2019	MIN	MLB	31	11	9	0	28	28	168	167	20	3.6	7.6	142	49%	.298

Breakout: 10% Improve: 39% Collapse: 29% Attrition: 9% MLB: 92%
Comparables: Yovani Gallardo, Andrew Cashner, Clay Buchholz

Of the 198 pitchers who threw 500 or more four-seam fastballs in 2018, Gibson had the second-lowest Called Strike Probability (CSProb) on those pitches. Of the 92 who threw at least 500 sinkers, he had the eighth-lowest CSProb. Of the 61 who threw at least 500 sliders, Gibson had the third-lowest CSProb. Almost no one in baseball is around the middle of the zone less often than Gibson, but his new formula is working. The four-seamer sets everything up and keeps opponents thinking about the whole zone, the sinker remains a worm-killer and the slider induced whiffs at by far the highest clip of his career. He walks more batters this way, but compared to the version of Gibson that tried to skate by with AstroTurf-era strikeout rates, he's way more effective.

YEAR	TEAM	LVL	AGE	WHIP	ERA	DRA	WARP	MPH	FB%	WHF	CSP
2016	MIN	MLB	28	1.56	5.07	6.31	-1.6	93.6	56.2	10.3	42.1
2017	ROC	AAA	29	1.04	2.08	2.75	0.6				
2017	MIN	MLB	29	1.53	5.07	5.20	0.7	94.4	56.7	10.6	42.2
2018	MIN	MLB	30	1.30	3.62	4.21	2.5	95.1	57.8	12.1	40.4
2019	MIN	MLB	31	1.40	4.16	4.57	1.7	93.7	56.8	11.2	41.2

Kyle Gibson, continued

Pitch Shape vs LHH

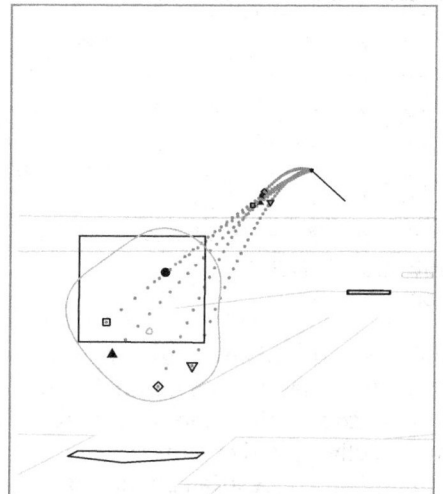

Pitch Shape vs RHH

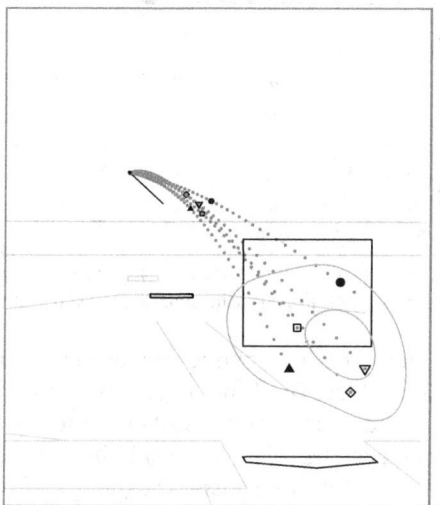

Type	Frequency	Velocity	H Movement	V Movement
● Fastball	23.8%	93.5 [103]	-4.7 [109]	-13.4 [107]
□ Sinker	33.9%	93.3 [104]	-12.3 [102]	-17.8 [108]
+ Cutter				
▲ Changeup	11.0%	86 [103]	-11.9 [97]	-28 [98]
× Splitter				
▽ Slider	21.0%	85.7 [106]	4.9 [100]	-33 [100]
◇ Curveball	10.2%	81 [109]	5.9 [92]	-44.4 [108]
⊕ Slow Curveball				
✴ Knuckleball				
▼ Screwball				

Stephen Gonsalves LHP

Born: 07/08/94   Age: 24   Bats: L   Throws: L
Height: 6'5"   Weight: 213   Origin: Round 4, 2013 Draft (#110 overall)

YEAR	TEAM	LVL	AGE	W	L	SV	G	GS	IP	H	HR	BB/9	K/9	K	GB%	BABIP
2016	FTM	A+	21	5	4	0	11	11	65^2	43	2	2.7	9.0	66	48%	.248
2016	CHT	AA	21	8	1	0	13	13	74^1	43	1	4.5	10.8	89	38%	.255
2017	CHT	AA	22	8	3	0	15	15	87^1	67	7	2.4	9.9	96	35%	.270
2017	ROC	AAA	22	1	2	0	5	4	22^2	27	4	3.2	8.7	22	34%	.343
2018	CHT	AA	23	3	0	0	4	4	20^1	11	2	4.4	11.1	25	51%	.231
2018	ROC	AAA	23	9	3	0	19	18	100^1	65	6	4.9	8.5	95	40%	.237
2018	MIN	MLB	23	2	2	0	7	4	24^2	28	2	8.0	5.8	16	40%	.321
2019	MIN	MLB	24	2	2	0	6	6	30	28	4	4.4	8.7	29	39%	.291

Breakout: 14%   Improve: 27%   Collapse: 32%   Attrition: 39%   MLB: 72%
Comparables: Keyvius Sampson, Henry Owens, Aaron Blair

Overpowering opponents was never going to be much of an option for Gonsalves. That's not to say that dominating them was beyond his ability: he racked up impressive strikeout rates at several stops in the minors. To do so, however, he relied on the ability to repeat his delivery and execute with extraordinary consistency, giving all four of his fairly pedestrian pitches the advantage of an assailant who was off balance. His command was nowhere near good enough to make all that work in 2018, however, especially after his arrival in the majors. Gonsalves threw his four-seamer 60 percent of the time in 2018; his path to big-league success is having enough confidence in the rest of his arsenal to shrink that number by half.

YEAR	TEAM	LVL	AGE	WHIP	ERA	DRA	WARP	MPH	FB%	WHF	CSP
2016	FTM	A+	21	0.96	2.33	3.02	1.8				
2016	CHT	AA	21	1.08	1.82	3.31	1.6				
2017	CHT	AA	22	1.03	2.68	3.07	2.2				
2017	ROC	AAA	22	1.54	5.56	4.13	0.4				
2018	CHT	AA	23	1.03	1.77	3.84	0.4				
2018	ROC	AAA	23	1.20	2.96	4.72	0.9				
2018	MIN	MLB	23	2.03	6.57	8.22	-0.9	92.1	59	6.9	48.3
2019	MIN	MLB	24	1.40	4.46	4.90	0.2	91.9	60.8	7.1	49.7

Stephen Gonsalves, continued

Pitch Shape vs LHH

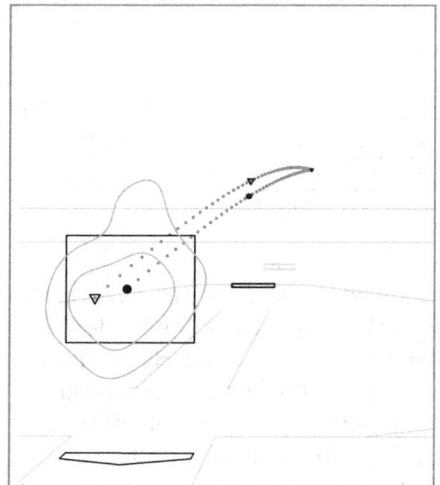

Pitch Shape vs RHH

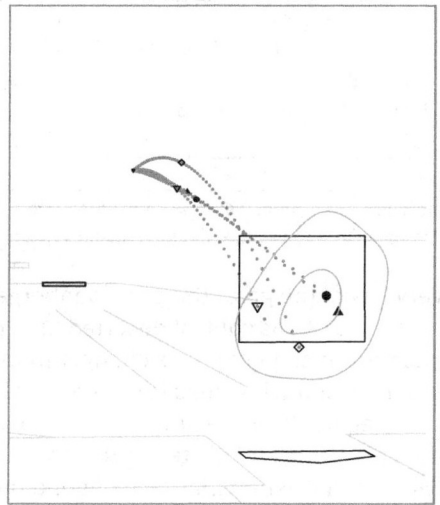

Type	Frequency	Velocity	H Movement	V Movement
● Fastball	59.0%	90.2 [93]	2.1 [121]	-14.5 [104]
☐ Sinker				
+ Cutter				
▲ Changeup	17.1%	82.1 [87]	7.5 [120]	-23.2 [112]
✕ Splitter				
▽ Slider	16.1%	84.8 [101]	-4.7 [99]	-29.8 [109]
◇ Curveball	7.8%	72.4 [77]	-9.6 [107]	-60.9 [71]
⊕ Slow Curveball				
✻ Knuckleball				
▼ Screwball				

Trevor Hildenberger   RHP
Born: 12/15/90   Age: 28   Bats: R   Throws: R
Height: 6'2"   Weight: 211   Origin: Round 22, 2014 Draft (#650 overall)

YEAR	TEAM	LVL	AGE	W	L	SV	G	GS	IP	H	HR	BB/9	K/9	K	GB%	BABIP
2016	FTM	A+	25	1	1	3	6	0	9^1	11	0	0.0	7.7	8	64%	.355
2016	CHT	AA	25	2	3	16	32	0	38^2	21	2	1.4	10.5	45	61%	.211
2017	ROC	AAA	26	2	1	6	21	0	30^2	27	1	2.3	10.3	35	56%	.321
2017	MIN	MLB	26	3	3	1	37	0	42	38	4	1.3	9.4	44	60%	.304
2018	MIN	MLB	27	4	6	7	73	0	73	75	12	3.2	8.6	70	48%	.301
2019	MIN	MLB	28	3	3	0	54	0	57	55	7	3.6	8.5	54	50%	.296

Breakout: 28%   Improve: 40%   Collapse: 27%   Attrition: 13%   MLB: 81%
Comparables: Ryan Dull, Pedro Baez, Matt Reynolds

Very few of the great things Hildenberger showed in his rookie campaign carried over to 2018. His control deserted him, largely because he lost the feel for both pitches (his sinker and his changeup) that move to the arm side. He did flash the grounder-inducing quasi-dominance of 2017 during the late spring and early summer, but he wore down from there and batters began sitting on his slider, then elevating and blistering it. At his best, Hildenberger is a four-pitch reliever with a non-existent platoon split and the command to consistently induce very weak contact, but it's possible the late bloomer's best is gone for good.

YEAR	TEAM	LVL	AGE	WHIP	ERA	DRA	WARP	MPH	FB%	WHF	CSP
2016	FTM	A+	25	1.18	0.96	3.03	0.2				
2016	CHT	AA	25	0.70	0.70	2.09	1.2				
2017	ROC	AAA	26	1.14	2.05	2.37	1.0				
2017	MIN	MLB	26	1.05	3.21	3.27	0.9	93.2	51	12.4	44.8
2018	MIN	MLB	27	1.38	5.42	5.28	-0.3	93.3	44.1	13.4	47.1
2019	MIN	MLB	28	1.36	4.13	4.47	0.4	92.7	46.5	13.2	46.3

Trevor Hildenberger, continued

Pitch Shape vs LHH

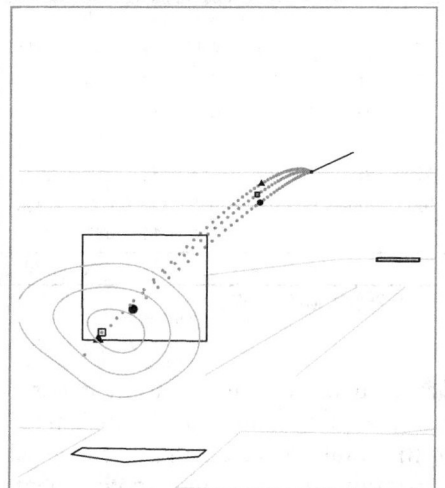

Pitch Shape vs RHH

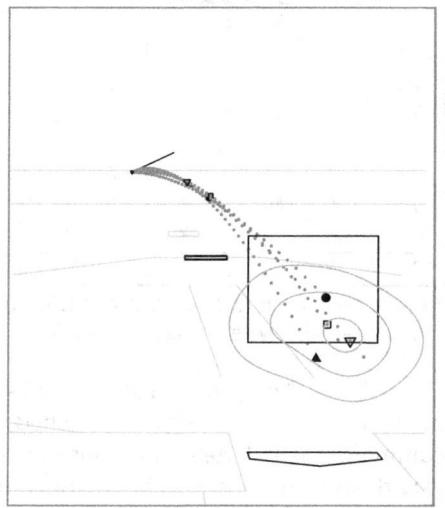

Type	Frequency	Velocity	H Movement	V Movement
● Fastball	7.7%	92.6 [100]	-11.4 [78]	-18.7 [91]
☐ Sinker	36.4%	89.3 [84]	-14.1 [88]	-31.4 [64]
+ Cutter				
▲ Changeup	32.9%	78.4 [72]	-10.7 [103]	-41.5 [58]
✕ Splitter				
▽ Slider	23.0%	78.7 [74]	5.8 [104]	-43 [70]
◇ Curveball				
⊕ Slow Curveball				
✲ Knuckleball				
▼ Screwball				

Zack Littell RHP

Born: 10/05/95 Age: 23 Bats: R Throws: R
Height: 6'4" Weight: 220 Origin: Round 11, 2013 Draft (#327 overall)

YEAR	TEAM	LVL	AGE	W	L	SV	G	GS	IP	H	HR	BB/9	K/9	K	GB%	BABIP
2016	CLN	A	20	5	5	0	16	16	97²	94	5	1.9	8.8	95	51%	.332
2016	BAK	A+	20	8	1	0	12	11	68	64	3	1.7	8.1	61	49%	.311
2017	TAM	A+	21	9	1	0	13	11	71¹	65	4	1.9	7.2	57	55%	.302
2017	TRN	AA	21	5	0	0	7	7	44	37	3	1.6	10.6	52	52%	.304
2017	CHT	AA	21	5	0	0	7	7	41²	33	1	3.9	7.1	33	55%	.274
2018	CHT	AA	22	0	3	0	5	5	23	28	3	2.7	12.5	32	38%	.431
2018	ROC	AAA	22	6	6	0	19	15	106	100	5	3.4	8.3	98	40%	.310
2018	MIN	MLB	22	0	2	0	8	2	20¹	25	3	4.9	6.2	14	44%	.319
2019	MIN	MLB	23	2	2	0	33	0	34	33	4	3.4	8.4	32	43%	.297

Breakout: 6% Improve: 15% Collapse: 12% Attrition: 25% MLB: 30%
Comparables: Abe Alvarez, David Holmberg, Brady Rodgers

The only good way to approach Littell's first taste of the majors is to treat it as a mulligan. Still tall, young and polished, with five pitches and the athleticism to command them, Littell retains his back-of-the-rotation upside. Pitchers of his ilk — with so many weapons but no obviously optimal way to deploy them — bear a bit more risk than others of simply never putting everything together. Littell's repertoire's depth is mitigated by the absence of any offering that projects to facilitate a move to the bullpen. Risk certainly lurks with Littell, and it swells with each unsuccessful start he makes, but it's too early to count him out.

YEAR	TEAM	LVL	AGE	WHIP	ERA	DRA	WARP	MPH	FB%	WHF	CSP
2016	CLN	A	20	1.18	2.76	3.64	1.6				
2016	BAK	A+	20	1.13	2.51	4.19	1.0				
2017	TAM	A+	21	1.12	1.77	4.32	0.8				
2017	TRN	AA	21	1.02	2.05	3.12	1.1				
2017	CHT	AA	21	1.22	2.81	3.98	0.6				
2018	CHT	AA	22	1.52	5.87	3.72	0.4				
2018	ROC	AAA	22	1.32	3.57	4.02	1.7				
2018	MIN	MLB	22	1.77	6.20	6.71	-0.4	94.6	58.5	8	49.2
2019	MIN	MLB	23	1.34	4.07	4.42	0.3	94.5	60.6	8.3	51

Zack Littell, continued

Pitch Shape vs LHH

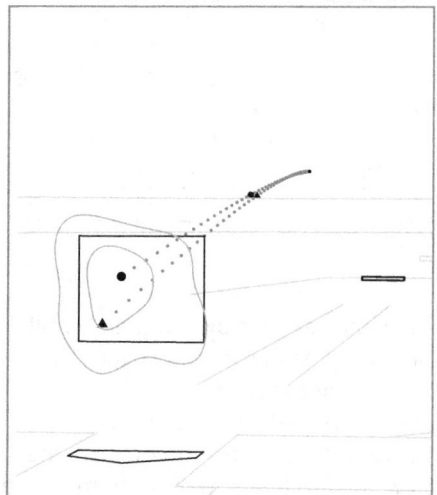

Pitch Shape vs RHH

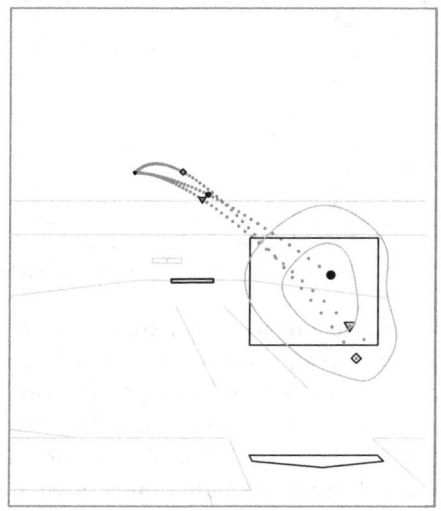

Type	Frequency	Velocity	H Movement	V Movement
● Fastball	50.0%	92.4 [100]	-6.1 [102]	-14.7 [103]
☐ Sinker	8.5%	91.5 [95]	-11.9 [106]	-18.6 [106]
+ Cutter				
▲ Changeup	11.5%	85.8 [102]	-13.3 [89]	-27.1 [101]
✕ Splitter				
▽ Slider	16.9%	86.9 [111]	3.3 [93]	-26.5 [119]
◇ Curveball	13.1%	75.1 [88]	8.2 [102]	-55.9 [82]
⊕ Slow Curveball				
✱ Knuckleball				
▼ Screwball				

Matt Magill   RHP

Born: 11/10/89   Age: 29   Bats: R   Throws: R
Height: 6'3"   Weight: 210   Origin: Round 31, 2008 Draft (#937 overall)

YEAR	TEAM	LVL	AGE	W	L	SV	G	GS	IP	H	HR	BB/9	K/9	K	GB%	BABIP
2016	PEN	AA	26	0	0	1	9	0	9^2	12	0	5.6	14.9	16	46%	.500
2016	LOU	AAA	26	4	1	0	29	0	42^1	40	6	4.5	9.1	43	44%	.306
2016	CIN	MLB	26	0	0	0	5	0	4^1	5	1	10.4	2.1	1	29%	.308
2017	ELP	AAA	27	6	5	0	19	17	95^2	105	13	3.9	6.9	73	45%	.316
2018	ROC	AAA	28	0	0	2	5	0	8^2	5	0	2.1	13.5	13	28%	.278
2018	MIN	MLB	28	3	3	0	40	0	56^2	58	11	3.7	8.9	56	35%	.301
2019	MIN	MLB	29	3	3	0	54	0	57	56	9	4.4	8.9	57	40%	.296

Breakout: 13%   Improve: 16%   Collapse: 13%   Attrition: 17%   MLB: 32%
Comparables: Dusty Hughes, Rob Scahill, Joe Savery

A minor-league journeyman, swingman and whack-a-mole big leaguer, Magill popped up for his longest stint in the majors throwing harder than ever. His mid-90s fastball is too straight and gets crushed, though, and he can't consistently throw strikes with his cutter or his curveball. He remains an extreme fly-ball guy, and is vulnerable to the long ball. By the end of 2018, the league brought its giant mallet down hard on Magill's head. In order to remain a useful reliever, he'll need to hone one of those breaking balls and continue the trend he used to survive September: throwing far fewer fastballs.

YEAR	TEAM	LVL	AGE	WHIP	ERA	DRA	WARP	MPH	FB%	WHF	CSP
2016	PEN	AA	26	1.86	6.52	1.58	0.4				
2016	LOU	AAA	26	1.44	4.46	3.48	0.7				
2016	CIN	MLB	26	2.31	6.23	6.54	-0.1	94.9	68.3	7.3	45.4
2017	ELP	AAA	27	1.53	3.95	4.81	0.9				
2018	ROC	AAA	28	0.81	0.00	2.67	0.2				
2018	MIN	MLB	28	1.43	3.81	5.42	-0.3	96.4	60.9	11.8	46
2019	MIN	MLB	29	1.46	4.92	5.08	0.0	95.7	61.2	11.6	45.8

Matt Magill, continued

Pitch Shape vs LHH

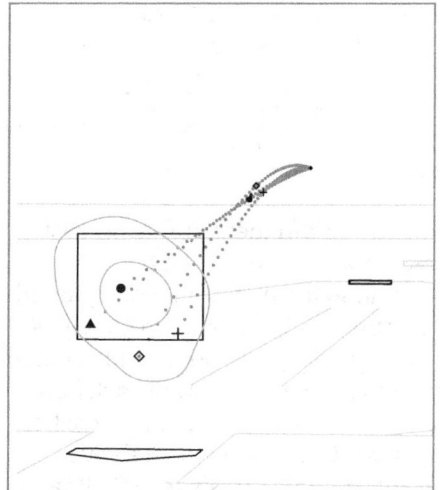

Pitch Shape vs RHH

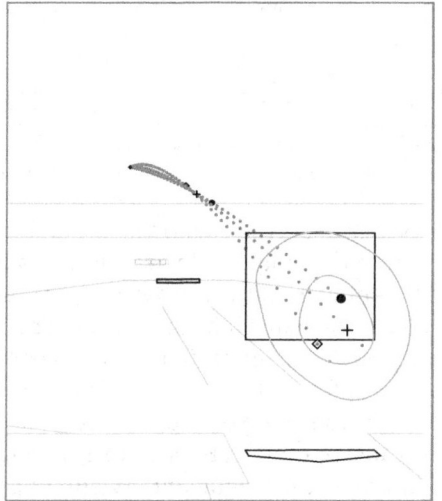

Type	Frequency	Velocity	H Movement	V Movement
● Fastball	60.8%	95 [108]	-6.6 [100]	-12.7 [110]
□ Sinker	0.1%	94.6 [111]	-14.4 [86]	-16.4 [113]
+ Cutter	18.2%	86.7 [88]	6 [124]	-30.2 [74]
▲ Changeup	3.6%	88.3 [112]	-12.4 [94]	-24.7 [108]
× Splitter				
▽ Slider	1.4%	85.1 [103]	9.1 [118]	-30.9 [106]
◇ Curveball	15.9%	84.8 [123]	4.1 [84]	-43.2 [111]
⊕ Slow Curveball				
✳ Knuckleball				
▼ Screwball				

Trevor May RHP

Born: 09/23/89 Age: 29 Bats: R Throws: R
Height: 6'5" Weight: 240 Origin: Round 4, 2008 Draft (#136 overall)

YEAR	TEAM	LVL	AGE	W	L	SV	G	GS	IP	H	HR	BB/9	K/9	K	GB%	BABIP
2016	MIN	MLB	26	2	2	0	44	0	42²	39	7	3.6	12.7	60	32%	.317
2018	ROC	AAA	28	0	4	2	13	4	27	24	2	5.3	8.3	25	40%	.293
2018	MIN	MLB	28	4	1	3	24	1	25¹	21	4	1.8	12.8	36	41%	.298
2019	MIN	MLB	29	3	3	22	54	0	57	51	6	4.1	10.1	64	39%	.298

Breakout: 29% Improve: 56% Collapse: 17% Attrition: 16% MLB: 84%
Comparables: Brett Cecil, Charlie Furbush, Joel Hanrahan

May has an average fastball, though it's played up from there during his past stints in the bullpen. He has a good changeup, though the movement differential from the fastball is almost all lateral, so it tends to generate ground balls more than whiffs (and when it's not executed well, batters can hit it a long way). His breaking stuff has always been a work in progress, but he did get more comfortable with his curveball last year even as he worked his way back from Tommy John surgery. Some modernization is in order for May's approach: he was absent from MLB for all of 2017 and most of 2018. During that relatively short time, the league underwent a significant shift toward fewer fastballs and more secondary pitches. May will benefit from mimicking that adjustment.

YEAR	TEAM	LVL	AGE	WHIP	ERA	DRA	WARP	MPH	FB%	WHF	CSP
2016	MIN	MLB	26	1.31	5.27	4.10	0.4	96.7	61	13.8	47.2
2018	ROC	AAA	28	1.48	4.00	3.55	0.5				
2018	MIN	MLB	28	1.03	3.20	2.98	0.6	95.5	59.2	15.6	46.7
2019	MIN	MLB	29	1.34	3.54	3.97	0.8	95.4	60.1	14.7	46.8

Trevor May, continued

Pitch Shape vs LHH

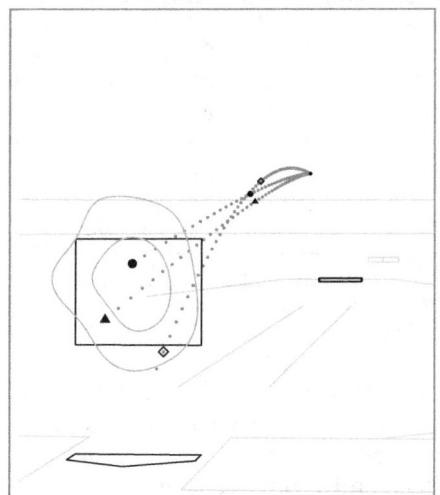

Pitch Shape vs RHH

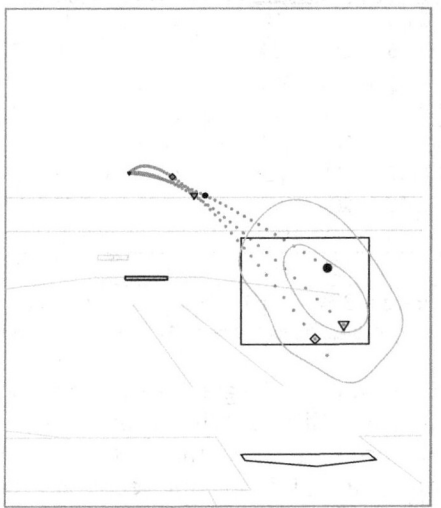

Type	Frequency	Velocity	H Movement	V Movement
● Fastball	59.2%	94.4 [106]	-4.7 [109]	-13.2 [108]
□ Sinker				
+ Cutter				
▲ Changeup	10.7%	86.1 [103]	-9.8 [108]	-19.6 [123]
× Splitter				
▽ Slider	10.7%	87.5 [113]	4.9 [100]	-29.8 [109]
◇ Curveball	19.4%	78.4 [100]	10.2 [110]	-50.8 [94]
⊕ Slow Curveball				
✳ Knuckleball				
▼ Screwball				

Adalberto Mejia LHP

Born: 06/20/93   Age: 26   Bats: R   Throws: L
Height: 6'3"   Weight: 195   Origin: International Free Agent, 2011

YEAR	TEAM	LVL	AGE	W	L	SV	G	GS	IP	H	HR	BB/9	K/9	K	GB%	BABIP
2016	RIC	AA	23	3	2	0	11	11	65	48	4	2.2	8.0	58	48%	.251
2016	SAC	AAA	23	4	1	0	7	7	40²	42	5	2.4	9.5	43	42%	.327
2016	MIN	MLB	23	0	0	0	1	0	2¹	5	0	3.9	0.0	0	42%	.417
2016	ROC	AAA	23	2	2	0	4	4	26¹	28	3	1.0	8.5	25	33%	.329
2017	ROC	AAA	24	1	1	0	6	6	28²	26	1	1.9	6.9	22	51%	.294
2017	MIN	MLB	24	4	7	0	21	21	98	110	13	4.0	7.8	85	41%	.328
2018	ROC	AAA	25	5	3	0	15	12	63¹	55	3	2.8	8.8	62	43%	.294
2018	MIN	MLB	25	2	0	0	5	4	22¹	17	1	3.6	5.2	13	40%	.239
2019	MIN	MLB	26	3	3	0	10	10	53	53	7	3.3	8.0	47	42%	.297

Breakout: 30%   Improve: 53%   Collapse: 18%   Attrition: 23%   MLB: 81%
Comparables: Trevor Williams, Andrew Heaney, Cody Anderson

Everywhere Mejia goes, frustration follows in his wake. He's blessed with a high-spin fastball, a hard, late-breaking slider and a fine changeup. He's never had great command, but the stuff should work better than it does. Mejia struggles to maintain a physique that keeps him balanced and strong on the mound, especially as he works past the first trip through the batting order. He doesn't even get ground balls, despite that mostly horizontal slider and a heavy sinker (a pitch he should, perhaps, throw more often). He's not embarrassingly out of shape, or a major makeup disaster, or a yips-afflicted wild horse. He's just a pitcher who seems like he should be decent but manages not to be.

YEAR	TEAM	LVL	AGE	WHIP	ERA	DRA	WARP	MPH	FB%	WHF	CSP
2016	RIC	AA	23	0.98	1.94	2.96	1.7				
2016	SAC	AAA	23	1.30	4.20	3.63	0.8				
2016	MIN	MLB	23	2.57	7.71	7.31	-0.1	93.2	45.2	7.1	45.8
2016	ROC	AAA	23	1.18	3.76	2.88	0.7				
2017	ROC	AAA	24	1.12	2.83	3.90	0.6				
2017	MIN	MLB	24	1.57	4.50	6.02	-0.5	94.2	56.3	11.2	43.6
2018	ROC	AAA	25	1.18	3.27	4.10	1.0				
2018	MIN	MLB	25	1.16	2.01	6.86	-0.4	94.6	59.1	9.5	48
2019	MIN	MLB	26	1.39	4.28	4.70	0.4	93.9	57.7	11	46.8

Adalberto Mejia, continued

Pitch Shape vs LHH

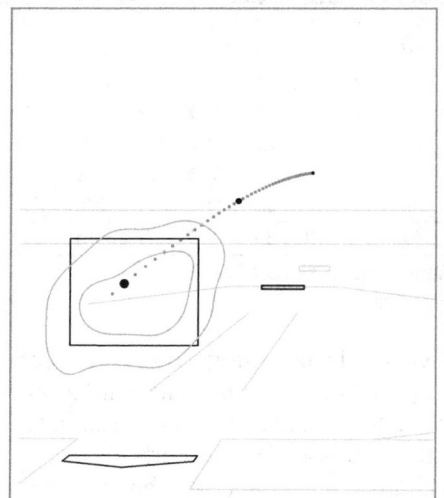

Pitch Shape vs RHH

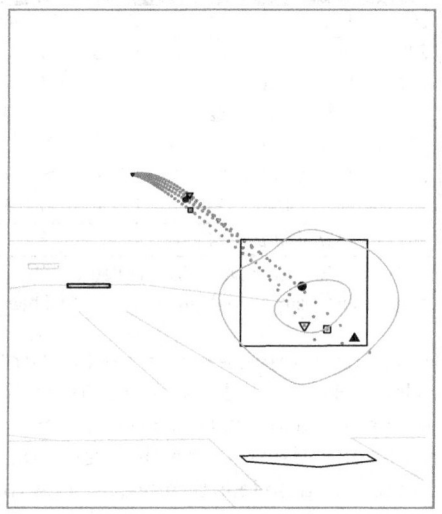

Type	Frequency	Velocity	H Movement	V Movement
● Fastball	45.4%	92.8 [101]	5.8 [104]	-14.3 [104]
□ Sinker	13.7%	91.5 [95]	12.5 [101]	-21.3 [97]
+ Cutter				
▲ Changeup	17.4%	81.9 [86]	12.7 [93]	-30.5 [91]
× Splitter				
▽ Slider	23.5%	85.3 [104]	-2.8 [91]	-31.3 [105]
◇ Curveball				
✣ Slow Curveball				
✳ Knuckleball				
▼ Screwball				

Gabriel Moya LHP

Born: 01/09/95   Age: 24   Bats: L   Throws: L
Height: 6'0"   Weight: 175   Origin: International Free Agent, 2012

YEAR	TEAM	LVL	AGE	W	L	SV	G	GS	IP	H	HR	BB/9	K/9	K	GB%	BABIP
2016	KNC	A	21	1	0	0	12	0	19	12	0	1.9	9.5	20	51%	.255
2016	VIS	A+	21	5	1	5	40	0	44²	26	2	2.6	12.5	62	41%	.255
2017	WTN	AA	22	4	1	17	34	0	43²	22	1	2.5	14.0	68	44%	.259
2017	CHT	AA	22	2	0	7	13	0	14²	8	1	1.8	11.7	19	44%	.212
2017	MIN	MLB	22	0	0	1	7	0	6¹	5	2	2.8	7.1	5	32%	.176
2018	ROC	AAA	23	1	1	4	26	4	42²	38	2	2.5	10.5	50	38%	.336
2018	MIN	MLB	23	3	1	0	35	6	36¹	35	6	3.2	7.7	31	40%	.269
2019	MIN	MLB	24	4	4	0	62	8	65	59	10	3.7	9.8	71	40%	.292

Breakout: 17%   Improve: 29%   Collapse: 18%   Attrition: 22%   MLB: 61%
Comparables: Cody Allen, Manny Delcarmen, Shae Simmons

Moya doesn't throw especially hard or have a truly nasty single pitch on which to lean. He succeeds, when he succeeds, by pitching as purely backward as any reliever in baseball. He would rather start a left-handed batter with a slider, or a right-handed one with a changeup, than throw them a fastball early in the count. When he falls behind, he uses the change to get back into the count or induce weak contact, even against fellow lefties. Then, he uses the fastball (which sits only in the low 90s) as his put-away pitch. That's a peculiar profile for a reliever, and it makes Moya tough to cast in a modern bullpen. He's not a matchup guy, per se, nor is he someone most teams want pitching full innings of high-leverage ball. Used as an opener at times in 2018, he does seem a good fit in that role.

YEAR	TEAM	LVL	AGE	WHIP	ERA	DRA	WARP	MPH	FB%	WHF	CSP
2016	KNC	A	21	0.84	0.47	2.53	0.5				
2016	VIS	A+	21	0.87	2.01	2.70	1.2				
2017	WTN	AA	22	0.78	0.82	2.19	1.4				
2017	CHT	AA	22	0.75	0.61	2.56	0.4				
2017	MIN	MLB	22	1.11	4.26	4.14	0.1	92.2	45.7	12.4	39.3
2018	ROC	AAA	23	1.17	1.90	2.56	1.3				
2018	MIN	MLB	23	1.32	4.71	5.74	-0.3	91.6	42	10.5	48.5
2019	MIN	MLB	24	1.31	4.14	4.49	0.5	91.5	43.7	11.1	45.8

Gabriel Moya, continued

Pitch Shape vs LHH

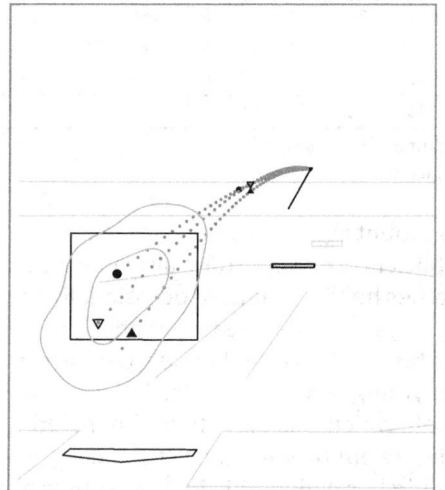

Pitch Shape vs RHH

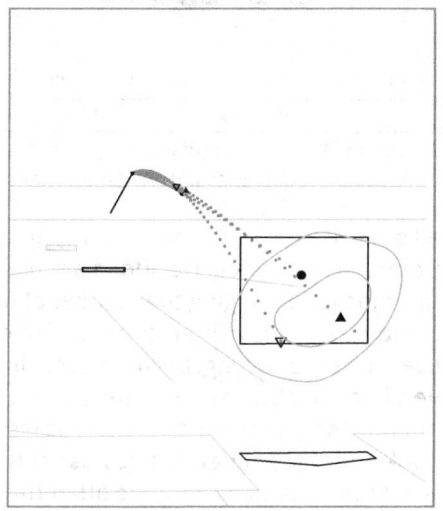

Type	Frequency	Velocity	H Movement	V Movement
● Fastball	35.6%	90 [92]	7.1 [98]	-16.2 [99]
☐ Sinker	6.4%	89.3 [84]	12.5 [101]	-20.4 [100]
+ Cutter				
▲ Changeup	39.6%	81.6 [85]	9.4 [110]	-29.8 [93]
✕ Splitter				
▽ Slider	11.8%	81.7 [87]	-2.2 [89]	-36 [91]
◇ Curveball	6.5%	79.6 [104]	-3.6 [82]	-42.1 [113]
⊕ Slow Curveball				
✻ Knuckleball				
▼ Screwball				

Twins Player Analysis - 71

Minnesota Twins 2019

Jake Odorizzi   RHP
Born: 03/27/90   Age: 29   Bats: R   Throws: R
Height: 6'2"   Weight: 190   Origin: Round 1, 2008 Draft (#32 overall)

YEAR	TEAM	LVL	AGE	W	L	SV	G	GS	IP	H	HR	BB/9	K/9	K	GB%	BABIP
2016	TBA	MLB	26	10	6	0	33	33	187²	170	29	2.6	8.0	166	38%	.271
2017	TBA	MLB	27	10	8	0	28	28	143¹	117	30	3.8	8.0	127	32%	.227
2018	MIN	MLB	28	7	10	0	32	32	164¹	151	20	3.8	8.9	162	31%	.290
2019	MIN	MLB	29	8	9	0	24	24	136	138	26	3.5	8.2	125	34%	.287

Breakout: 17%   Improve: 44%   Collapse: 20%   Attrition: 7%   MLB: 95%
Comparables: Edwin Jackson, Steve Carlton, Yovani Gallardo

All over MLB, 2018 saw sinkers disappear. Count that as another way in which Odorizzi is an outlier. He added a sinker back into his repertoire after being dealt to Minnesota, bringing the number of pitches he threw at least occasionally to six: four-seamer, splitter, curve, slider, cutter, sinker. He needs that ability to keep hitters guessing, because ever since his splitter ceased to be a bat-misser, he's been unable to consistently throw anything past opponents. Odorizzi pounds the top of the zone with his fastball, which sets up both his improved hook and that splitter, but he has yet to figure out how to induce the weak contact he's seeking with the other three pitches. Vulnerable to deep counts and short outings, he'll blossom if allowed to work behind an opener and avoid facing the meat of opposing lineups for a third time.

YEAR	TEAM	LVL	AGE	WHIP	ERA	DRA	WARP	MPH	FB%	WHF	CSP
2016	TBA	MLB	26	1.19	3.69	4.88	1.0	94.1	60	10.7	45.7
2017	TBA	MLB	27	1.24	4.14	5.29	0.5	93.4	48.7	12.1	43.9
2018	MIN	MLB	28	1.34	4.49	5.62	-0.6	92.8	54.3	11.7	42.1
2019	MIN	MLB	29	1.38	4.89	5.36	0.1	92.7	54.2	11.5	43.6

Jake Odorizzi, continued

Pitch Shape vs LHH

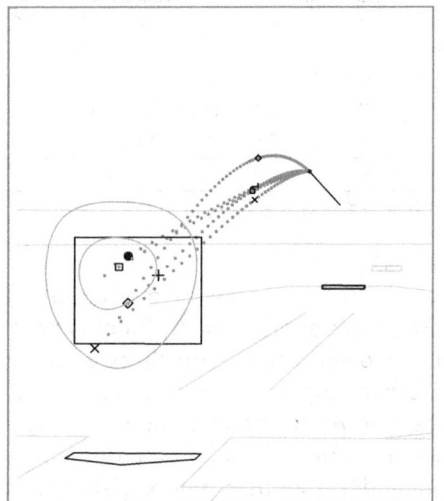

Pitch Shape vs RHH

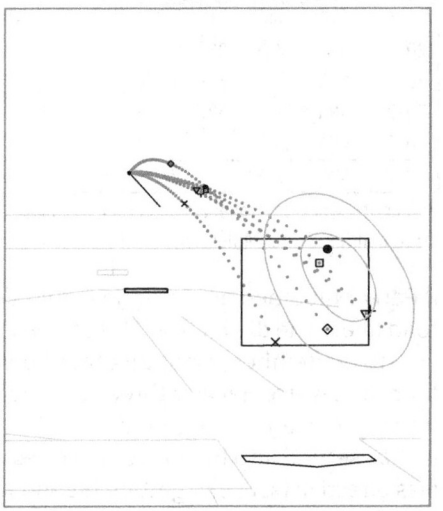

Type	Frequency	Velocity	H Movement	V Movement
● Fastball	35.1%	91.3 [96]	-7.1 [98]	-13.8 [106]
□ Sinker	19.2%	91.3 [94]	-10.4 [118]	-15.8 [115]
+ Cutter	10.5%	85.1 [78]	5 [118]	-25.2 [94]
▲ Changeup	0.9%	83.6 [93]	-9.1 [112]	-27.7 [99]
× Splitter	16.5%	84.5 [93]	-9.9 [93]	-27.1 [110]
▽ Slider	12.9%	83 [93]	6.6 [107]	-30.2 [108]
◇ Curveball	4.9%	72.8 [79]	8.5 [103]	-57.1 [80]
⊕ Slow Curveball				
✳ Knuckleball				
▼ Screwball				

Blake Parker   RHP

Born: 06/19/85   Age: 34   Bats: R   Throws: R
Height: 6'3"   Weight: 225   Origin: Round 16, 2006 Draft (#479 overall)

YEAR	TEAM	LVL	AGE	W	L	SV	G	GS	IP	H	HR	BB/9	K/9	K	GB%	BABIP
2016	TAC	AAA	31	1	2	19	38	0	39^2	24	4	2.5	12.7	56	44%	.256
2016	SEA	MLB	31	0	0	0	1	0	1	1	0	9.0	0.0	0	75%	.250
2016	NYA	MLB	31	1	0	1	16	0	16^1	16	1	4.4	8.3	15	49%	.312
2017	ANA	MLB	32	3	3	8	71	0	67^1	40	7	2.1	11.5	86	48%	.229
2018	ANA	MLB	33	2	1	14	67	0	66^1	63	12	2.6	9.5	70	35%	.297
2019	MIN	MLB	34	3	3	4	54	0	57	54	9	3.4	9.5	61	41%	.294

Breakout: 14%   Improve: 27%   Collapse: 31%   Attrition: 9%   MLB: 80%
Comparables: Justin Miller, Tyler Walker, Kiko Calero

If Parker bloomed any later he would be a toad lily. You know the deal about toad lilies: The distinctive white flower with purple spots typically blooms from July to September just as all other flowers are beginning to fade. Since being a four-time waiver pickup three years ago, Parker has thrown the vast majority of his major league innings in the last two seasons. As he enters his age-34 season, he has settled into high-leverage roles via fiery baptism. His fastball became way less effective last year, getting hit and launched further than before, perhaps signifying his bloom is near its end. Toad lily, we hardly knew ye.

YEAR	TEAM	LVL	AGE	WHIP	ERA	DRA	WARP	MPH	FB%	WHF	CSP
2016	TAC	AAA	31	0.88	2.72	1.72	1.5				
2016	SEA	MLB	31	2.00	0.00	12.02	-0.1	94.4	73.1	7.7	50
2016	NYA	MLB	31	1.47	4.96	4.44	0.1	94.2	55.8	11.9	45.3
2017	ANA	MLB	32	0.83	2.54	2.26	2.2	95.0	60	15.1	44.7
2018	ANA	MLB	33	1.24	3.26	5.19	-0.2	94.0	57.5	11.6	46.5
2019	MIN	MLB	34	1.32	4.20	4.52	0.4	93.3	57.6	12.8	45

Blake Parker, continued

Pitch Shape vs LHH
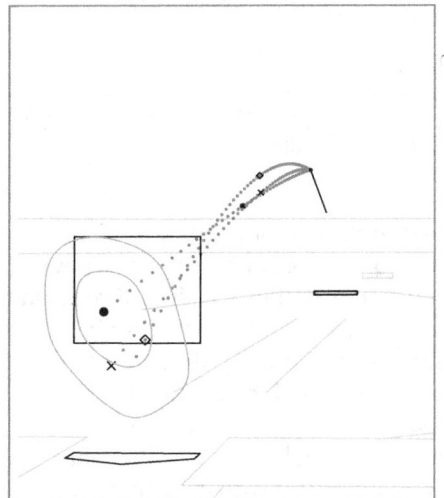

Pitch Shape vs RHH
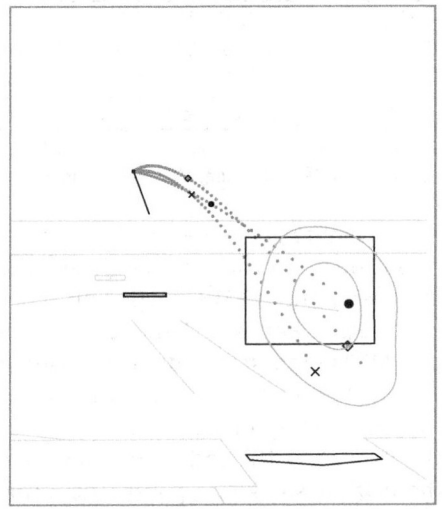

Type	Frequency	Velocity	H Movement	V Movement
● Fastball	57.5%	92.8 [101]	-4.1 [112]	-14 [105]
□ Sinker				
+ Cutter				
▲ Changeup				
✕ Splitter	31.2%	81 [74]	-7.7 [102]	-37.6 [66]
▽ Slider	0.7%	88.6 [118]	3.7 [95]	-26.2 [120]
◇ Curveball	10.7%	78.1 [99]	5.9 [92]	-49.7 [96]
⊕ Slow Curveball				
✳ Knuckleball				
▼ Screwball				

Martin Perez LHP
Born: 04/04/91   Age: 28   Bats: L   Throws: L
Height: 6'0"   Weight: 200   Origin: International Free Agent, 2007

YEAR	TEAM	LVL	AGE	W	L	SV	G	GS	IP	H	HR	BB/9	K/9	K	GB%	BABIP
2016	TEX	MLB	25	10	11	0	33	33	198^2	205	18	3.4	4.7	103	54%	.286
2017	TEX	MLB	26	13	12	0	32	32	185	221	23	3.1	5.6	115	48%	.328
2018	TEX	MLB	27	2	7	0	22	15	85^1	116	16	3.8	5.5	52	52%	.344
2019	MIN	MLB	28	6	6	0	19	19	100^2	109	13	3.6	6.1	69	50%	.302

Breakout: 17%   Improve: 54%   Collapse: 19%   Attrition: 14%   MLB: 97%
Comparables: Matt Harrison, Mike Pelfrey, John Lannan

If you want to give Perez the benefit of the doubt, you could point to the offseason injury in which a bull knocked him off a fence and suggest he never quite felt right in 2018, despite his repeated claims that he was fine. If you don't want to give Perez the benefit of the doubt, you could point to his mediocre pre-2018 numbers and put the finishing touches on your "Ferdinand was Framed" posters. The most frustrating part about watching Perez pitch is not that he's bad, but that he's pretty good about 70 percent of the time. Unfortunately, the bad is *really* bad: a four-run inning here, a six-run inning there. It's like baking a gourmet cupcake and topping it with icing (not too rich), those really tasty sugar sprinkles that add taste *and* texture, plus one tiiiiiiiny little squirt of poisoned frog blood. Sure, most of it was delicious, but now you're in the hospital, and half of your face is paralyzed. The good news for Perez? He's left-handed, under 30 and the cupcakes are good enough to take a risk that he's figured out how to keep the frogs (and bulls) out of his kitchen.

YEAR	TEAM	LVL	AGE	WHIP	ERA	DRA	WARP	MPH	FB%	WHF	CSP
2016	TEX	MLB	25	1.41	4.39	6.09	-1.7	95.4	61.7	8.8	45.2
2017	TEX	MLB	26	1.54	4.82	7.09	-3.1	95.0	58.7	8	41.1
2018	TEX	MLB	27	1.78	6.22	7.31	-2.0	95.1	67.3	8.2	48.8
2019	MIN	MLB	28	1.51	4.55	4.98	0.5	94.6	62.1	8.3	45.6

Martin Perez, continued

Pitch Shape vs LHH

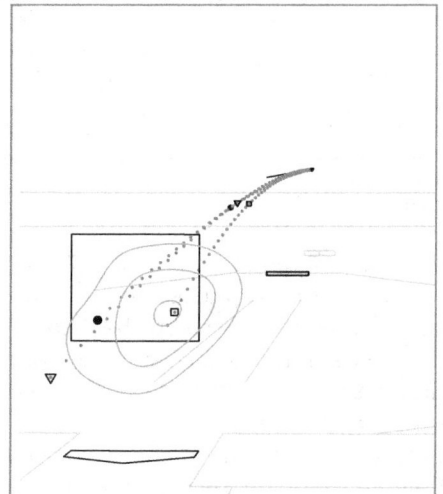

Pitch Shape vs RHH

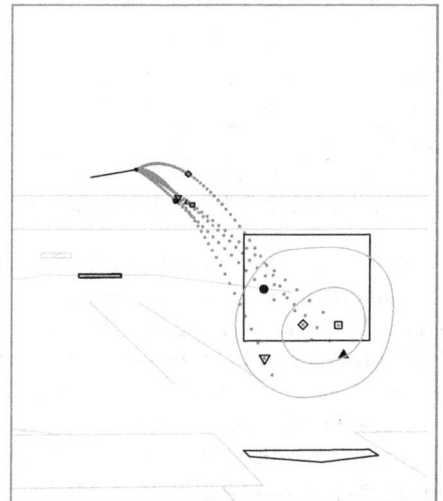

Type	Frequency	Velocity	H Movement	V Movement
● Fastball	16.5%	93.2 [102]	8.4 [92]	-14.6 [104]
☐ Sinker	50.7%	93.1 [103]	14.8 [82]	-19.7 [102]
+ Cutter				
▲ Changeup	17.2%	84.7 [97]	13.3 [89]	-25.3 [106]
✕ Splitter				
▽ Slider	6.8%	84 [98]	-3.2 [93]	-33.2 [99]
◇ Curveball	8.6%	78.3 [99]	-6.1 [93]	-46 [105]
✦ Slow Curveball				
✲ Knuckleball				
▼ Screwball				

Addison Reed   RHP

Born: 12/27/88   Age: 30   Bats: L   Throws: R
Height: 6'4"   Weight: 230   Origin: Round 3, 2010 Draft (#95 overall)

YEAR	TEAM	LVL	AGE	W	L	SV	G	GS	IP	H	HR	BB/9	K/9	K	GB%	BABIP
2016	NYN	MLB	27	4	2	1	80	0	77^2	60	4	1.5	10.5	91	42%	.286
2017	NYN	MLB	28	1	2	19	48	0	49	49	6	1.1	8.8	48	38%	.307
2017	BOS	MLB	28	1	1	0	29	0	27	16	5	3.0	9.3	28	47%	.175
2018	MIN	MLB	29	1	6	0	55	0	56	65	11	2.4	7.1	44	32%	.320
2019	MIN	MLB	30	3	3	8	54	0	57	60	10	3.3	8.0	51	38%	.295

Breakout: 22%   Improve: 53%   Collapse: 22%   Attrition: 8%   MLB: 90%
Comparables: Hoyt Wilhelm, Jeff Montgomery, Joe Sambito

Since 1947, 22 pitchers have appeared in at least 150 total games at ages 27 and 28. That might seem to mark extreme usage, but since the pitchers in this pool were already into their prime and physically mature, they've mostly held up better than one might expect. Sixteen of the first 21 pitched at least 100 innings across their age-29 and age-30 seasons, and most of them remained well above average. Reed, however, had a miserable 2018, and all signs point to fatigue, undiagnosed injury or some mixture of the two as the driving force. His velocity dropped precipitously, and his fastball straightened out in a way that made him far too easy to square up. There's no credible basis on which to project that his stuff will return to the level that allowed him to enjoy such success in the middle of the decade.

YEAR	TEAM	LVL	AGE	WHIP	ERA	DRA	WARP	MPH	FB%	WHF	CSP
2016	NYN	MLB	27	0.94	1.97	2.58	2.1	94.8	72.2	13.6	54
2017	NYN	MLB	28	1.12	2.57	3.86	0.7	93.7	69.1	13.5	55.2
2017	BOS	MLB	28	0.93	3.33	2.48	0.8	94.6	62.3	16.3	46.2
2018	MIN	MLB	29	1.43	4.50	5.61	-0.4	93.1	70.2	11.9	50.7
2019	MIN	MLB	30	1.41	5.05	5.18	0.0	93.2	69.2	13.3	51.8

Addison Reed, continued

Pitch Shape vs LHH	Pitch Shape vs RHH
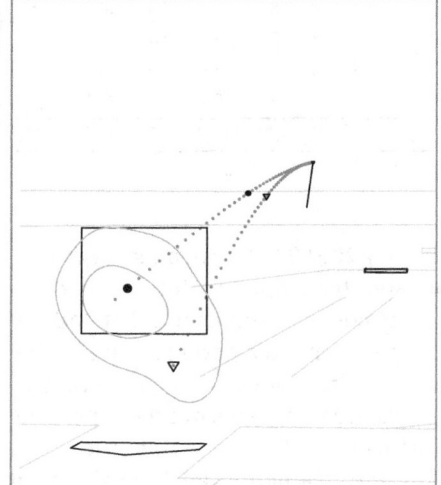	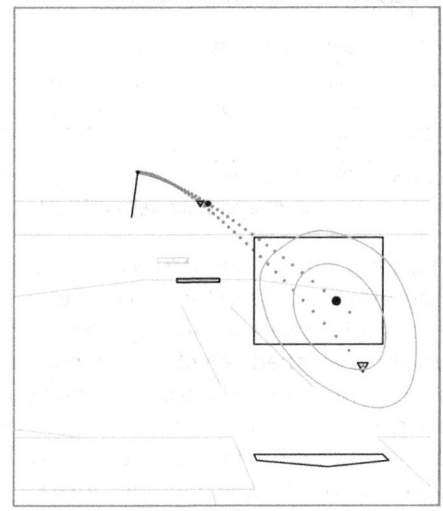

Type	Frequency	Velocity	H Movement	V Movement
● Fastball	68.1%	91.3 [96]	-0.2 [130]	-15.5 [101]
☐ Sinker	2.0%	89.7 [86]	-9.7 [124]	-18.4 [106]
+ Cutter				
▲ Changeup				
✕ Splitter				
▽ Slider	29.8%	84.3 [99]	5.7 [104]	-30.7 [107]
◇ Curveball				
⊕ Slow Curveball				
✻ Knuckleball				
▼ Screwball				

Taylor Rogers LHP

Born: 12/17/90   Age: 28   Bats: L   Throws: L
Height: 6'3"   Weight: 170   Origin: Round 11, 2012 Draft (#340 overall)

YEAR	TEAM	LVL	AGE	W	L	SV	G	GS	IP	H	HR	BB/9	K/9	K	GB%	BABIP
2016	ROC	AAA	25	0	1	0	7	2	18	24	1	3.0	7.5	15	44%	.365
2016	MIN	MLB	25	3	1	0	57	0	61^1	63	7	2.3	9.4	64	51%	.326
2017	MIN	MLB	26	7	3	0	69	0	55^2	52	6	3.4	7.9	49	46%	.291
2018	MIN	MLB	27	1	2	2	72	0	68^1	49	3	2.1	9.9	75	46%	.280
2019	MIN	MLB	28	3	3	3	54	0	57	51	6	3.4	9.8	63	46%	.302

Breakout: 22%   Improve: 43%   Collapse: 22%   Attrition: 18%   MLB: 87%
Comparables: Jose Alvarez, Blake Treinen, Troy Patton

Opposing hitters managed a pitcheresque .147/.206/.231 line against Rogers from June 1 through the end of the season, and that's not an arbitrarily drawn line. Starting very late in May, Rogers added a slider to a repertoire that had previously leaned heavily on an unimpressive sinker and a good curveball. The slider turned out to be a devastating partner in crime for the hook, such that by the end of the year, he was throwing one of his breaking balls nearly 60 percent of the time without the slightest loss of effectiveness. TrackMan rules the baseball world these days, because it makes improvements like Rogers' not only possible but repeatable, and often permanent.

YEAR	TEAM	LVL	AGE	WHIP	ERA	DRA	WARP	MPH	FB%	WHF	CSP
2016	ROC	AAA	25	1.67	4.50	3.33	0.4				
2016	MIN	MLB	25	1.29	3.96	4.28	0.5	95.0	55.2	8	50.5
2017	MIN	MLB	26	1.31	3.07	4.63	0.3	94.7	62.3	9.3	50
2018	MIN	MLB	27	0.95	2.63	3.33	1.3	95.2	52.9	12.3	51.5
2019	MIN	MLB	28	1.29	3.27	3.74	0.9	94.4	56.8	10.3	51

Taylor Rogers, continued

Pitch Shape vs LHH

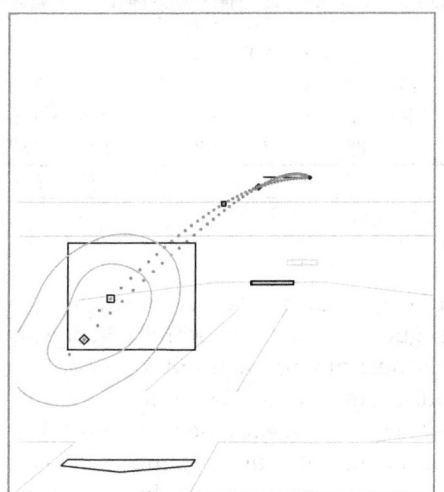

Pitch Shape vs RHH

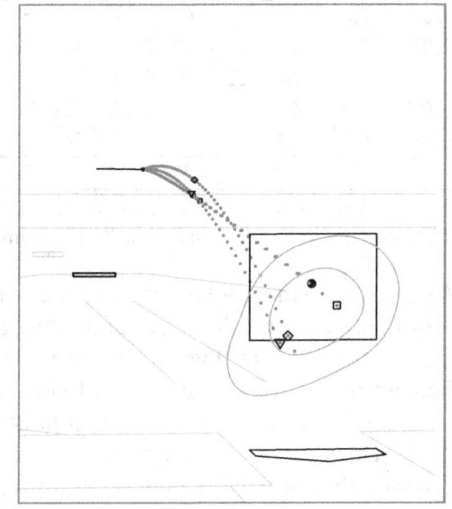

Type	Frequency	Velocity	H Movement	V Movement
● Fastball	5.3%	94 [105]	12 [76]	-17.3 [95]
☐ Sinker	47.6%	93.7 [106]	15 [80]	-20.5 [100]
+ Cutter				
▲ Changeup	0.6%	89.6 [117]	16.2 [74]	-28.9 [95]
× Splitter				
▽ Slider	13.2%	83.7 [97]	-8 [114]	-32.7 [101]
◇ Curveball	33.3%	78.6 [101]	-13.7 [125]	-42.3 [113]
⊕ Slow Curveball				
✳ Knuckleball				
▼ Screwball				

Fernando Romero RHP

Born: 12/24/94   Age: 24   Bats: R   Throws: R
Height: 6'0"   Weight: 215   Origin: International Free Agent, 2011

YEAR	TEAM	LVL	AGE	W	L	SV	G	GS	IP	H	HR	BB/9	K/9	K	GB%	BABIP
2016	CDR	A	21	4	1	0	5	5	28	18	0	1.6	8.0	25	53%	.250
2016	FTM	A+	21	5	2	0	11	11	62^1	48	1	1.4	9.4	65	58%	.288
2017	CHT	AA	22	11	9	0	24	23	125	124	4	3.2	8.6	120	54%	.328
2018	MIN	MLB	23	3	3	0	11	11	55^2	60	6	3.1	7.3	45	48%	.318
2018	ROC	AAA	23	5	6	0	16	13	90^2	85	5	3.2	6.8	69	50%	.294
2019	MIN	MLB	24	3	3	0	8	8	42	44	6	3.3	7.6	36	48%	.297

Breakout: 14%   Improve: 35%   Collapse: 12%   Attrition: 31%   MLB: 65%
Comparables: Alex Sanabia, Chad Kuhl, Paul Maholm

A classic case of a rookie learning the hard way what success in The Show requires, Romero's first taste of the big leagues looked really promising, only to crash and burn after five strong starts. At issue: Romero's attempt to rely on a heavy sinker as an equal partner to his four-seam fastball. He's more comfortable with the pitch, with aiming at low targets, with the matchup of his natural arm slot and the movement of the sinker. Unfortunately, the pitch just doesn't differentiate itself enough from his firm changeup or his sharp slider to make it (or them) effective. If he has a future in a big-league rotation, it's with that power sinker way up his sleeve. If he has a future in the bullpen, it might be as a turbo-sinker specialist.

YEAR	TEAM	LVL	AGE	WHIP	ERA	DRA	WARP	MPH	FB%	WHF	CSP
2016	CDR	A	21	0.82	1.93	3.31	0.6				
2016	FTM	A+	21	0.93	1.88	2.92	1.8				
2017	CHT	AA	22	1.35	3.53	3.79	2.0				
2018	MIN	MLB	23	1.42	4.69	6.13	-0.5	97.1	63.3	11.3	48.4
2018	ROC	AAA	23	1.29	3.57	4.14	1.4				
2019	MIN	MLB	24	1.42	4.32	4.74	0.3	96.9	65.2	11.6	49.9

Fernando Romero, continued

Pitch Shape vs LHH

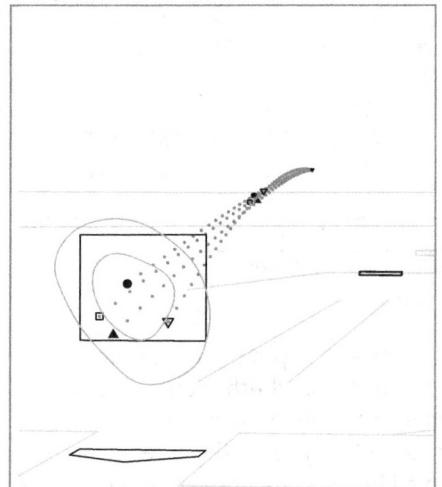

Pitch Shape vs RHH

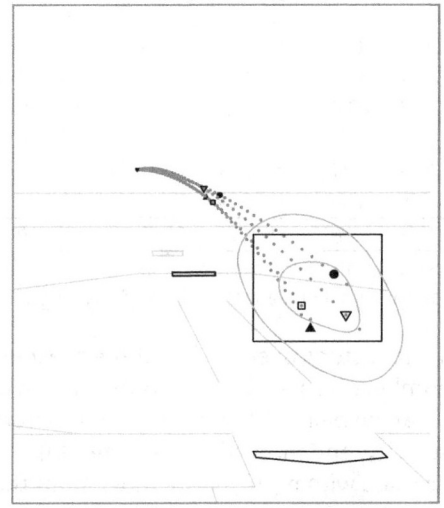

Type	Frequency	Velocity	H Movement	V Movement
● Fastball	31.1%	95.8 [111]	-7.8 [95]	-16 [99]
□ Sinker	32.2%	95.7 [116]	-14.1 [87]	-21.5 [96]
+ Cutter				
▲ Changeup	12.0%	90.6 [121]	-12.6 [93]	-26.5 [102]
× Splitter				
▽ Slider	24.7%	87.1 [112]	2.3 [89]	-32.3 [102]
◇ Curveball				
⊕ Slow Curveball				
✳ Knuckleball				
▼ Screwball				

Andrew Vasquez LHP
Born: 09/14/93   Age: 25   Bats: L   Throws: L
Height: 6'6"   Weight: 228   Origin: Round 32, 2015 Draft (#950 overall)

YEAR	TEAM	LVL	AGE	W	L	SV	G	GS	IP	H	HR	BB/9	K/9	K	GB%	BABIP
2016	ELZ	RK	22	2	0	0	4	0	10	6	0	3.6	13.5	15	67%	.333
2016	CDR	A	22	1	0	1	13	0	28^1	13	0	3.8	11.4	36	64%	.210
2017	CDR	A	23	1	0	0	14	0	22^1	15	0	4.0	13.3	33	70%	.326
2017	FTM	A+	23	3	1	2	23	0	35^2	32	0	2.8	13.1	52	62%	.390
2018	FTM	A+	24	0	2	5	19	0	32^2	24	1	3.6	10.2	37	60%	.280
2018	CHT	AA	24	1	0	0	17	1	31	21	1	1.2	17.1	59	50%	.408
2018	MIN	MLB	24	1	0	0	9	0	5	5	0	3.6	12.6	7	57%	.357
2019	MIN	MLB	25	1	1	0	27	0	28^2	25	3	4.7	10.3	33	51%	.304

Breakout: 21%   Improve: 27%   Collapse: 4%   Attrition: 26%   MLB: 40%
Comparables: Donnie Joseph, Shawn Armstrong, Dan Runzler

In eight stops over the last three seasons, Vasquez has put up video-game numbers (especially strikeouts) everywhere but MLB. Whether one calls his breaking ball a slider (it's pretty firm, relative to his below-average sinker velocity, and most of its movement is horizontal) or a curve (it's a really big breaker, with more lateral movement than all but a couple dozen other hurlers' breaking pitches), the pitch is nasty, and minor leaguers were consistently overmatched. In the big leagues, however, batters laid off it more often, and Vasquez didn't demonstrate the ability to throw it for a strike the way one must in order to succeed with his approach. His sinker has as much run as the curve has sweep, which can make it tough for him to remain deceptive against polished hitters and umpires who won't expand the plate. If he can firm up his command, though, he can make that a non-issue.

YEAR	TEAM	LVL	AGE	WHIP	ERA	DRA	WARP	MPH	FB%	WHF	CSP
2016	ELZ	RK	22	1.00	0.90	1.86	0.4				
2016	CDR	A	22	0.88	1.59	2.32	0.8				
2017	CDR	A	23	1.12	1.61	3.05	0.5				
2017	FTM	A+	23	1.21	1.51	2.53	1.0				
2018	FTM	A+	24	1.13	1.38	5.92	-0.4				
2018	CHT	AA	24	0.81	1.16	0.77	1.5				
2018	MIN	MLB	24	1.40	5.40	4.48	0.0	92.5	34.7	11.9	42.9
2019	MIN	MLB	25	1.43	3.71	4.11	0.3	92.2	35.5	12.2	43.9

Andrew Vasquez, continued

Pitch Shape vs LHH

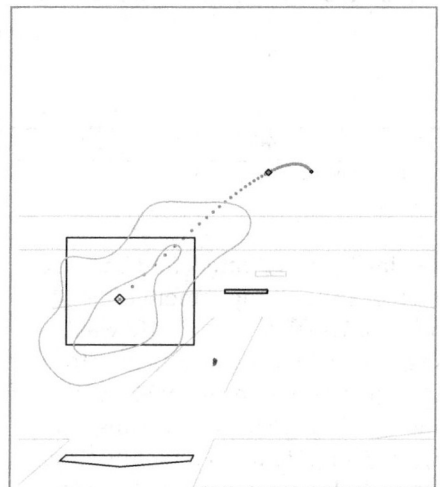

Pitch Shape vs RHH

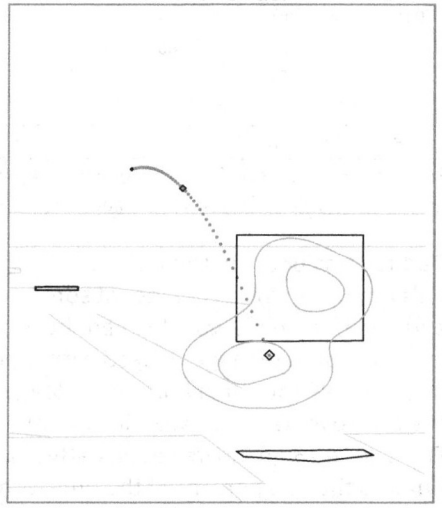

Type	Frequency	Velocity	H Movement	V Movement
● Fastball				
☐ Sinker	34.7%	90.4 [90]	15.2 [78]	-22.8 [92]
+ Cutter				
▲ Changeup	1.0%	84.3 [96]	14.6 [82]	-37.9 [69]
× Splitter				
▽ Slider				
◇ Curveball	64.4%	82.3 [114]	-13.6 [124]	-41.3 [115]
⊕ Slow Curveball				
✱ Knuckleball				
▼ Screwball				

Akil Baddoo CF

Born: 08/16/98 Age: 20 Bats: L Throws: L
Height: 5'11" Weight: 195 Origin: Round 2, 2016 Draft (#74 overall)

YEAR	TEAM	LVL	AGE	PA	R	2B	3B	HR	RBI	BB	K	SB	CS	AVG/OBP/SLG
2016	TWI	RK	17	128	15	0	2	2	15	18	36	8	1	.178/.299/.271
2017	TWI	RK	18	86	18	4	3	1	10	9	13	4	0	.267/.360/.440
2017	ELZ	RK	18	157	39	15	2	3	19	27	19	5	4	.357/.478/.579
2018	CDR	A	19	517	83	22	11	11	40	74	124	24	5	.243/.351/.419
2019	MIN	MLB	20	251	25	8	1	6	20	22	78	4	1	.139/.212/.267

Breakout: 7% Improve: 9% Collapse: 0% Attrition: 5% MLB: 9%
Comparables: Kyle Tucker, Billy McKinney, Victor Robles

Baddoo has been on the fast track since the day he was drafted, and because he's not Mike Trout, that meant some version of serious adjustment difficulty awaited him on his way through the low minors. The first half of 2018 was exactly that. A teenager tasked with figuring out his long swing and how to apply ample tools in a full-season league, Baddoo fanned roughly 30 percent of the time over the first two-plus months, and was limited by a hamstring injury. From June 16 on, however, he batted .263/.344/.449. He walked plenty, struck out less than 20 percent of the time, drove the ball to the gaps and became a terror on the bases. The ability to hang in there when challenged and to adjust that quickly make Baddoo a potential star.

YEAR	TEAM	LVL	AGE	PA	DRC+	VORP	BABIP	BRR	FRAA	WARP
2016	TWI	RK	17	128	74	-0.6	.243	0.2	RF(23): -0.5, CF(11): -3.2	-0.8
2017	TWI	RK	18	86	143	4.4	.311	0.9	CF(8): -0.7	0.2
2017	ELZ	RK	18	157	212	26.4	.400	0.8	CF(28): -4.2	1.2
2018	CDR	A	19	517	116	30.7	.311	4.7	CF(97): -12.1, LF(3): 0.1	1.0
2019	MIN	MLB	20	251	26	-12.4	.173	0.5	CF -4, LF 0	-1.8

Jason Castro C

Born: 06/18/87 Age: 32 Bats: L Throws: R
Height: 6'3" Weight: 215 Origin: Round 1, 2008 Draft (#10 overall)

YEAR	TEAM	LVL	AGE	PA	R	2B	3B	HR	RBI	BB	K	SB	CS	AVG/OBP/SLG
2016	HOU	MLB	29	376	41	16	3	11	32	45	123	2	1	.210/.307/.377
2017	MIN	MLB	30	407	49	22	0	10	47	45	108	0	0	.242/.333/.388
2018	MIN	MLB	31	74	4	3	0	1	3	9	26	0	0	.143/.257/.238
2019	MIN	MLB	32	327	34	15	1	8	33	34	92	1	0	.226/.312/.368

Breakout: 3% Improve: 37% Collapse: 15% Attrition: 22% MLB: 91%
Comparables: Brandon Inge, John Buck, Jason LaRue

The second season of Castro's three-year deal with Minnesota was over almost before it began. He got off to a sluggish but typical start, hitting poorly but showing good enough plate discipline to at least make pitchers work, and continuing to frame pitches well behind the plate. When he went under the knife to have a portion of the torn meniscus in his knee removed, however, the surgeon decided Castro needed a full repair instead. That meant stretching the rehabilitation period from several weeks to several months, and Castro's a catcher and this is a knee injury, so it might stretch his true recovery period from a few months to eternity.

YEAR	TEAM	P. COUNT	FRM RUNS	BLK RUNS	THRW RUNS	TOT RUNS
2016	HOU	14976	18.5	0.0	-0.9	17.4
2017	MIN	14556	8.3	0.3	-0.2	8.1
2018	MIN	3132	1.4	0.9	0.1	2.2
2019	MIN	12563	8.4	0.3	-0.6	8.0

YEAR	TEAM	LVL	AGE	PA	DRC+	VORP	BABIP	BRR	FRAA	WARP
2016	HOU	MLB	29	376	83	7.4	.297	-1.3	C(111): 18.0, 1B(3): -0.2	2.7
2017	MIN	MLB	30	407	86	13.0	.318	-0.4	C(108): 7.7	2.1
2018	MIN	MLB	31	74	57	-2.3	.216	-0.7	C(19): 2.5	0.2
2019	MIN	MLB	32	327	86	9.5	.305	-0.5	C 6	1.4

Minnesota Twins 2019

Gilberto Celestino CF
Born: 02/13/99 Age: 20 Bats: R Throws: L
Height: 6'0" Weight: 170 Origin: International Free Agent, 2015

YEAR	TEAM	LVL	AGE	PA	R	2B	3B	HR	RBI	BB	K	SB	CS	AVG/OBP/SLG
2016	DAR	ROK	17	165	22	9	3	2	17	25	23	9	2	.279/.388/.434
2016	AST	RK	17	65	7	3	1	0	2	8	16	6	1	.200/.308/.291
2017	GRV	RK	18	261	38	10	2	4	24	22	59	10	2	.268/.331/.379
2018	TCV	A-	19	142	18	8	0	4	21	10	25	14	0	.323/.387/.480
2018	ELZ	RK	19	117	13	4	1	1	13	6	16	8	2	.266/.308/.349
2019	MIN	MLB	20	251	24	6	0	6	19	9	74	4	1	.159/.187/.258

Breakout: 1% Improve: 1% Collapse: 0% Attrition: 0% MLB: 1%
Comparables: Engel Beltre, Carlos Tocci, Cedric Hunter

When a team pays the kind of money the Astros paid Celestino in 2015, they're quietly hoping for a rapid breakout, a race up the minor-league ladder that culminates in a big-league debut before the guy turns 21. Those are extremely rare cases, though, and Celestino's career to date is still a positive outcome. He's flashed gap power, offensive polish, top-end speed and great instincts both afield and on the bases. He's advancing slowly, but by no means old for his level, and if he can start to put these pieces of a great profile together, he'll see his prospect stock rise rapidly. Celestino still has two or three tough tests of player development to pass, however, before things get serious.

YEAR	TEAM	LVL	AGE	PA	DRC+	VORP	BABIP	BRR	FRAA	WARP
2016	DAR	ROK	17	165	151	12.6	.316	-0.8		1.1
2016	AST	RK	17	65	63	0.5	.275	-0.2	CF(16): -4.0	-0.7
2017	GRV	RK	18	261	102	13.6	.339	5.3	CF(43): 2.6, RF(8): 0.1	0.8
2018	TCV	A-	19	142	168	15.2	.374	1.6	CF(16): 0.9, RF(12): 2.6	1.2
2018	ELZ	RK	19	117	87	-0.8	.301	1.1	CF(23): -1.0	-0.1
2019	MIN	MLB	20	251	15	-16.8	.196	0.3	CF 0, RF 0	-1.8

Nick Gordon SS

Born: 10/24/95 Age: 23 Bats: L Throws: R
Height: 6'0" Weight: 160 Origin: Round 1, 2014 Draft (#5 overall)

YEAR	TEAM	LVL	AGE	PA	R	2B	3B	HR	RBI	BB	K	SB	CS	AVG/OBP/SLG
2016	FTM	A+	20	494	56	23	6	3	52	23	87	19	13	.291/.335/.386
2017	CHT	AA	21	578	80	29	8	9	66	53	134	13	7	.270/.341/.408
2018	CHT	AA	22	181	22	10	3	5	20	11	27	7	2	.333/.381/.525
2018	ROC	AAA	22	410	40	13	4	2	29	23	82	13	3	.212/.262/.283
2019	MIN	MLB	23	74	8	3	1	2	7	4	19	1	1	.232/.274/.391

Breakout: 28%   Improve: 41%   Collapse: 1%   Attrition: 33%   MLB: 44%
Comparables: Orlando Calixte, Yairo Munoz, Tim Beckham

If Tom was Flash and Gordon's brother Dee is Flash Jr., that still leaves Flash in the Pan as an available sobriquet, and the youngest Gordon in pro ball is circling it. He teases and inches toward real improvement every season, but the second half always seems to be a step backward. Gordon flashed power in his second trip through the Southern League, but a promotion to Triple-A saw the bat knocked out of his hands and a part-time move to second base. Though excruciatingly protracted, his development is by no means over. Gordon just needs to find a way to turn his foot speed into greater adjustment speed, because if he takes this long to adapt when he sees big-league pitching, he'll come to embody the original meaning of that new nickname: a misfire.

YEAR	TEAM	LVL	AGE	PA	DRC+	VORP	BABIP	BRR	FRAA	WARP
2016	FTM	A+	20	494	113	25.2	.353	-2.9	SS(103): 4.1, 2B(2): -0.1	1.7
2017	CHT	AA	21	578	116	34.0	.347	1.1	SS(104): 0.4, 2B(14): 0.4	2.4
2018	CHT	AA	22	181	139	13.8	.366	-1.4	SS(34): 2.4, 2B(6): -0.3	1.2
2018	ROC	AAA	22	410	53	-7.1	.264	2.8	SS(69): 2.6, 2B(30): 4.1	-0.1
2019	MIN	MLB	23	74	37	-2.7	.273	0.1	SS 0, 2B 1	-0.2

Alex Kirilloff   RF

Born: 11/09/97   Age: 21   Bats: L   Throws: L
Height: 6'2"   Weight: 195   Origin: Round 1, 2016 Draft (#15 overall)

YEAR	TEAM	LVL	AGE	PA	R	2B	3B	HR	RBI	BB	K	SB	CS	AVG/OBP/SLG
2016	ELZ	RK	18	232	33	9	1	7	33	11	32	0	1	.306/.341/.454
2018	CDR	A	20	281	36	20	5	13	56	24	47	1	1	.333/.391/.607
2018	FTM	A+	20	280	39	24	2	7	45	14	39	3	2	.362/.393/.550
2019	MIN	MLB	21	251	20	9	1	8	28	4	60	0	0	.197/.207/.340

Breakout: 15%   Improve: 25%   Collapse: 1%   Attrition: 15%   MLB: 28%
Comparables: Nomar Mazara, Jorge Bonifacio, Caleb Gindl

Confined to an outfield corner, Kirilloff has to hit for considerable power in order to deliver high-end value once he attains the majors. He demonstrated the potential to do just that in his return season from Tommy John surgery, blasting out 71 extra-base hits across the two least hitter-friendly full-season leagues in the minors. He also made plenty of contact and sprayed line drives all over the field. Kirilloff's midseason promotion to High-A was very aggressive, and his approach got a little less controlled there, but he still showed preternatural raw hitting talent. He'll get a chance to pass the Double-A test at 21, which would mean fully making up for the lost year of development, and all he needs to remember is to work for and punish his pitch.

YEAR	TEAM	LVL	AGE	PA	DRC+	VORP	BABIP	BRR	FRAA	WARP
2016	ELZ	RK	18	232	111	8.6	.328	0.8	RF(39): 5.2, CF(12): -2.7	0.3
2018	CDR	A	20	281	163	27.2	.364	-0.8	RF(53): -4.0, CF(1): 0.0	1.5
2018	FTM	A+	20	280	163	26.9	.399	-0.8	RF(51): 0.4, CF(3): 0.3	1.7
2019	MIN	MLB	21	251	40	-11.9	.223	-0.4	RF -2, CF 0	-1.4

Trevor Larnach OF

Born: 02/26/97   Age: 22   Bats: L   Throws: R
Height: 6'4"   Weight: 210   Origin: Round 1, 2018 Draft (#20 overall)

YEAR	TEAM	LVL	AGE	PA	R	2B	3B	HR	RBI	BB	K	SB	CS	AVG/OBP/SLG
2018	ELZ	RK	21	75	10	5	0	2	16	10	11	2	0	.311/.413/.492
2018	CDR	A	21	102	17	8	1	3	10	11	17	1	0	.297/.373/.505
2019	MIN	MLB	22	251	22	12	0	7	28	14	60	0	0	.197/.239/.345

Breakout: 2%   Improve: 6%   Collapse: 1%   Attrition: 4%   MLB: 6%
Comparables: Jorge Bonifacio, Destin Hood, Billy McKinney

One of the clearest and most valuable lessons of the systematic study of baseball, from a baseball ops perspective, is that everyone should be drafting polished collegiate hitters more aggressively. Larnach has every tool but speed, and his power came on in a big way during his junior year at College World Series-winning Oregon State. He's a huge left-handed hitter with a solid approach and a gorgeous swing, and he won't hurt you in either outfield corner. He went out as a pro and smoothly swatted around low-minors pitching. That the Twins got him for well below slot value at the 20th pick in the first round is a reminder of how far many teams have to go in optimizing their draft strategies.

YEAR	TEAM	LVL	AGE	PA	DRC+	VORP	BABIP	BRR	FRAA	WARP
2018	ELZ	RK	21	75	168	5.4	.340	-1.5	RF(14): 3.8	0.6
2018	CDR	A	21	102	150	8.8	.338	0.7	RF(17): -1.5	0.5
2019	MIN	MLB	22	251	49	-9.1	.229	-0.4	RF 0	-1.0

Royce Lewis SS
Born: 06/05/99   Age: 20   Bats: R   Throws: R
Height: 6'2"   Weight: 188   Origin: Round 1, 2017 Draft (#1 overall)

YEAR	TEAM	LVL	AGE	PA	R	2B	3B	HR	RBI	BB	K	SB	CS	AVG/OBP/SLG
2017	TWI	RK	18	159	38	6	2	3	17	19	17	15	2	.271/.390/.414
2017	CDR	A	18	80	16	2	1	1	10	6	16	3	1	.296/.363/.394
2018	CDR	A	19	327	50	23	0	9	53	24	49	22	4	.315/.368/.485
2018	FTM	A+	19	208	33	6	3	5	21	19	35	6	4	.255/.327/.399
2019	MIN	MLB	20	251	27	5	0	7	21	11	60	5	2	.188/.228/.299

Breakout: 20%   Improve: 23%   Collapse: 0%   Attrition: 5%   MLB: 23%
Comparables: Alen Hanson, Carlos Correa, J.P. Crawford

The first half of 2018 looked like a sure step on the path to superstardom for the top pick in the 2017 draft. The second half looked like a sideways step for an extremely polished and talented teenager who nonetheless has a lot to learn on his way to the majors. There's nothing wrong with the latter, unless one got carried away by the former. All five tools grade out well for Lewis, but none threaten the top of the scale. His aptitude and work ethic draw rave reviews, so there's always a chance his hit, power or glove plays up slightly. In the meantime, he'll ascend to Double-A, needing to demonstrate a bit more consistency but with plenty on which to build.

YEAR	TEAM	LVL	AGE	PA	DRC+	VORP	BABIP	BRR	FRAA	WARP
2017	TWI	RK	18	159	158	17.3	.292	4.6	SS(32): -0.9	1.2
2017	CDR	A	18	80	110	6.5	.364	1.0	SS(17): 1.9	0.6
2018	CDR	A	19	327	152	31.3	.349	3.7	SS(67): 0.8	3.2
2018	FTM	A+	19	208	106	11.6	.291	1.7	SS(45): -4.8	0.3
2019	MIN	MLB	20	251	39	-8.5	.219	0.3	SS -1	-1.0

Brent Rooker   LF

Born: 11/01/94   Age: 24   Bats: R   Throws: R
Height: 6'3"   Weight: 215   Origin: Round 1, 2017 Draft (#35 overall)

YEAR	TEAM	LVL	AGE	PA	R	2B	3B	HR	RBI	BB	K	SB	CS	AVG/OBP/SLG
2017	ELZ	RK	22	99	19	5	0	7	17	11	21	2	2	.282/.364/.588
2017	FTM	A+	22	162	23	6	0	11	35	16	47	0	0	.280/.364/.552
2018	CHT	AA	23	568	72	32	4	22	79	56	150	6	1	.254/.333/.465
2019	MIN	MLB	24	251	30	10	1	11	30	17	80	0	0	.200/.258/.393

Breakout: 18%   Improve: 31%   Collapse: 5%   Attrition: 31%   MLB: 53%
Comparables: Chris Shaw, Scott Schebler, Corey Dickerson

Unapologetically focused on lifting and driving the ball, Rooker is more popular on Baseball Twitter than craft beer. Like craft beer, however, Rooker's commitment to a niche forces him to excel in certain areas. His 2018 campaign failed to prove conclusively that he's a future 35-homer slugger in the majors, but it *did* shatter any lingering dreams that he would be a useful fielder or baserunner. There's no shortage of power or patience here, but because his future impact hinges on both things translating neatly to the majors, the questions around him can't be answered until he sees big-league pitching for half a season or more.

YEAR	TEAM	LVL	AGE	PA	DRC+	VORP	BABIP	BRR	FRAA	WARP
2017	ELZ	RK	22	99	140	10.0	.288	0.6	LF(17): 0.4	0.4
2017	FTM	A+	22	162	160	12.9	.341	-1.5	LF(16): -2.6, 1B(11): -0.4	0.4
2018	CHT	AA	23	568	116	13.2	.316	-4.7	1B(47): -5.7, LF(44): -8.2	-1.2
2019	MIN	MLB	24	251	74	-2.4	.250	-0.2	1B -2, LF -3	-0.8

Ben Rortvedt C
Born: 09/25/97   Age: 21   Bats: L   Throws: R
Height: 5'10"   Weight: 190   Origin: Round 2, 2016 Draft (#56 overall)

YEAR	TEAM	LVL	AGE	PA	R	2B	3B	HR	RBI	BB	K	SB	CS	AVG/OBP/SLG
2016	TWI	RK	18	66	3	3	0	0	3	5	8	0	0	.203/.277/.254
2016	ELZ	RK	18	47	2	0	0	0	7	5	2	0	0	.250/.348/.250
2017	CDR	A	19	336	33	16	0	4	30	22	60	1	0	.224/.284/.315
2018	CDR	A	20	157	14	9	2	1	16	10	35	1	0	.276/.325/.386
2018	FTM	A+	20	196	20	7	1	4	27	21	29	0	0	.250/.337/.372
2019	MIN	MLB	21	251	18	5	0	5	21	9	59	0	0	.153/.185/.241

Breakout: 10%   Improve: 11%   Collapse: 0%   Attrition: 8%   MLB: 11%
Comparables: Carson Kelly, Reese McGuire, Christian Vazquez

The biggest problem with catching prospects — for the team, and for the prospects themselves — is that they tend to develop slowly. That means, with only extraordinary exceptions, a catcher will blossom into a viable big leaguer both at and behind the plate only just in time to slip him onto the 40-man roster, and if he becomes a star, it might not be for long, and he might be halfway out the door when it happens. For that reason, teams invest less in catching than they might, and we outsiders see that reflected in the evaluations of backstops. Rortvedt is a perfect example. An advanced hitter coming out of high school, he's slowed down at the plate, but he's figuring out receiving well. His approach is steady, though so far he's short on power. For a catcher, he's advancing pretty quickly.

YEAR	TEAM	LVL	AGE	PA	DRC+	VORP	BABIP	BRR	FRAA	WARP
2016	TWI	RK	18	66	85	-1.1	.235	-1.8	C(17): 0.4	-0.1
2016	ELZ	RK	18	47	102	2.6	.263	0.1	C(13): 0.1	0.1
2017	CDR	A	19	336	72	3.0	.265	-1.1	C(86): 1.3	0.0
2018	CDR	A	20	157	114	6.2	.355	1.1	C(29): 1.0	0.8
2018	FTM	A+	20	196	97	10.2	.279	-0.4	C(45): -0.4	0.3
2019	MIN	MLB	21	251	10	-16.7	.176	-0.5	C 0	-1.8

Jorge Alcala RHP

Born: 07/28/95 Age: 23 Bats: R Throws: R
Height: 6'3" Weight: 180 Origin: International Free Agent, 2014

YEAR	TEAM	LVL	AGE	W	L	SV	G	GS	IP	H	HR	BB/9	K/9	K	GB%	BABIP
2016	AST	RK	20	1	1	1	6	3	22^1	14	0	2.4	14.1	35	71%	.311
2016	GRV	RK	20	2	1	0	6	4	20	12	0	3.6	9.0	20	55%	.245
2016	TCV	A-	20	0	1	0	3	3	13^2	20	1	2.6	9.9	15	49%	.432
2017	QUD	A	21	2	0	0	6	4	31	16	3	3.5	10.2	35	51%	.194
2017	BCA	A+	21	5	6	0	16	14	78^1	55	7	3.8	6.9	60	40%	.223
2018	BCA	A+	22	1	4	2	10	7	38^2	25	2	4.2	10.5	45	48%	.256
2018	CCH	AA	22	2	3	1	9	5	40^2	36	1	3.8	8.2	37	42%	.307
2018	CHT	AA	22	0	4	0	5	4	20	23	4	6.3	9.9	22	35%	.339
2019	MIN	MLB	23	4	5	1	34	13	82^1	79	12	4.9	8.7	79	43%	.294

Breakout: 13% Improve: 20% Collapse: 13% Attrition: 29% MLB: 40%
Comparables: Brooks Brown, Shawn Morimando, Bobby Livingston

What Alcala is depends entirely upon what you believe his miserable numbers after a midseason trade mean. In one reading, the fact that the Astros (with an analytical savvy that far outstrips that of any other team, one that has served them just as well in player development as in talent acquisition) gave up on Alcala might signal he's doomed never to find one good breaking ball among the two undistinguished ones he throws right now. In another, it might be a normal blip in the transition of a very talented pitching prospect to a new organization. Alcala's pro career has been spent in the rotation, but his future is in the bullpen, where his too-firm changeup isn't a problem and he can lean on just his high-90s heat and his slider. This season should see his first prolonged audition for that role.

YEAR	TEAM	LVL	AGE	WHIP	ERA	DRA	WARP	MPH	FB%	WHF	CSP
2016	AST	RK	20	0.90	1.21	1.42	1.0				
2016	GRV	RK	20	1.00	1.80	2.67	0.6				
2016	TCV	A-	20	1.76	5.27	2.80	0.4				
2017	QUD	A	21	0.90	2.03	2.79	0.9				
2017	BCA	A+	21	1.12	3.45	4.47	0.7				
2018	BCA	A+	22	1.11	3.03	3.35	0.9				
2018	CCH	AA	22	1.30	3.54	4.12	0.5				
2018	CHT	AA	22	1.85	5.85	5.08	0.0				
2019	MIN	MLB	23	1.51	5.11	5.36	-0.1				

Jhoan Duran RHP

Born: 01/08/98   Age: 21   Bats: R   Throws: R
Height: 6'5"   Weight: 175   Origin: International Free Agent, 2014

YEAR	TEAM	LVL	AGE	W	L	SV	G	GS	IP	H	HR	BB/9	K/9	K	GB%	BABIP
2016	DIA	RK	18	1	2	0	4	4	20	24	1	2.2	5.8	13	55%	.354
2016	MSO	RK	18	0	1	0	3	3	12^2	14	1	3.6	6.4	9	49%	.283
2017	DIA	RK	19	0	2	0	3	3	11^1	19	0	3.2	10.3	13	64%	.452
2017	YAK	A-	19	6	3	0	11	11	51	44	5	3.0	6.4	36	54%	.253
2018	KNC	A	20	5	4	0	15	15	64^2	69	6	3.9	9.9	71	52%	.346
2018	CDR	A	20	2	1	0	6	6	36	19	2	2.5	11.0	44	66%	.218
2019	MIN	MLB	21	4	6	0	16	16	75^1	81	10	4.6	7.6	63	47%	.308

Breakout: 5%   Improve: 9%   Collapse: 3%   Attrition: 10%   MLB: 14%
Comparables: Jarrod Parker, Patrick Corbin, Jarred Cosart

To bet on Duran is to bet on his changeup, and to bet on his changeup is an appealing proposition once you watch his delivery. He can ramp his fastball up into the high 90s in bursts, but it sits in the 95 mph range with life. Duran already possesses a curveball that flashes better than average, and has confidence in it. He's carved up the lower minors. The next step will be to see whether he can firm up his command, which can be loose within the zone. As with any pitching prospect yet to face advanced hitters and with the repertoire still in development, there's tons of risk here. If things fall together well, though, Duran will bloom into either a mid-rotation starter or a fiendish back-end reliever.

YEAR	TEAM	LVL	AGE	WHIP	ERA	DRA	WARP	MPH	FB%	WHF	CSP
2016	DIA	RK	18	1.45	5.85	4.33	0.3				
2016	MSO	RK	18	1.50	3.55	9.57	-0.5				
2017	DIA	RK	19	2.03	7.15	5.61	0.1				
2017	YAK	A-	19	1.20	4.24	4.32	0.6				
2018	KNC	A	20	1.50	4.73	3.51	1.3				
2018	CDR	A	20	0.81	2.00	2.51	1.1				
2019	MIN	MLB	21	1.58	5.09	5.34	0.1				

Blayne Enlow   RHP

Born: 03/21/99   Age: 20   Bats: R   Throws: R
Height: 6'3"   Weight: 170   Origin: Round 3, 2017 Draft (#76 overall)

YEAR	TEAM	LVL	AGE	W	L	SV	G	GS	IP	H	HR	BB/9	K/9	K	GB%	BABIP
2017	TWI	RK	18	3	0	0	6	1	20^1	10	1	1.8	8.4	19	56%	.176
2018	CDR	A	19	3	5	1	20	17	94	94	4	3.4	6.8	71	47%	.315
2019	MIN	MLB	20	3	4	0	25	10	63	76	13	4.9	6.1	43	44%	.309

Comparables: Robert Gsellman, James Parr, Raul Alcantara

Though he's yet to have any significant arm trouble, Enlow can't seem to stay healthy. He's gotten into a serious car accident in high school, slowing his pre-draft progress. In his first full pro season, he suffered ankle and back tweaks that sidelined him for several starts, though those recovery timetables were shaped by the Twins' preference to play it safe. After all, Enlow was already a teenager pitching in the Midwest League. When he was able to take the mound, however, he more than acquitted himself. With a fastball and a curve that each look to be plus offerings and a changeup he can throw for strikes when he needs to, Enlow will probably take the fastest track his body will permit. His size and mechanics suggest that he can stick in the rotation as he does so.

YEAR	TEAM	LVL	AGE	WHIP	ERA	DRA	WARP	MPH	FB%	WHF	CSP
2017	TWI	RK	18	0.69	1.33	2.53	0.7				
2018	CDR	A	19	1.37	3.26	4.36	0.9				
2019	MIN	MLB	20	1.74	6.44	6.79	-1.5				

Brusdar Graterol   RHP

Born: 08/26/98   Age: 20   Bats: R   Throws: R
Height: 6'1"   Weight: 180   Origin: International Free Agent, 2014

YEAR	TEAM	LVL	AGE	W	L	SV	G	GS	IP	H	HR	BB/9	K/9	K	GB%	BABIP
2017	TWI	RK	18	2	0	0	5	2	19^1	10	1	1.9	9.8	21	58%	.205
2017	ELZ	RK	18	2	1	0	5	5	20^2	16	1	3.9	10.5	24	59%	.300
2018	CDR	A	19	3	2	0	8	8	41^1	30	3	2.0	11.1	51	64%	.270
2018	FTM	A+	19	5	2	0	11	11	60^2	59	0	2.8	8.3	56	49%	.343
2019	MIN	MLB	20	4	5	0	15	15	71^1	73	10	4.3	8.3	65	50%	.308

Breakout: 4%   Improve: 5%   Collapse: 1%   Attrition: 3%   MLB: 6%
Comparables: Brad Keller, Will Smith, Jenrry Mejia

Some caution is in order where Graterol is concerned, because he won't turn 21 until August and he already has an elbow scar. His sheer stuff and ability to bully opposing batters tempted the Twins into a midseason level bump, and if he's not yet on the fast track he's one lane over from it. His fastball can touch 100 mph, and it's not without some wiggle. Pairing that with his plus slider would already make Graterol a holy terror in some future bullpen, but his arm action on the changeup gives him a chance to be more. Anything like ace status is off the table until he tightens his command, but he can already throw enough strikes to project as a mid-rotation hurler and an unhappy at-bat.

YEAR	TEAM	LVL	AGE	WHIP	ERA	DRA	WARP	MPH	FB%	WHF	CSP
2017	TWI	RK	18	0.72	1.40	2.83	0.6				
2017	ELZ	RK	18	1.21	3.92	3.76	0.5				
2018	CDR	A	19	0.94	2.18	3.57	0.8				
2018	FTM	A+	19	1.29	3.12	4.21	0.8				
2019	MIN	MLB	20	1.50	4.92	5.16	0.3				

Michael Pineda   RHP

Born: 01/18/89   Age: 30   Bats: R   Throws: R
Height: 6'7"   Weight: 260   Origin: International Free Agent, 2005

YEAR	TEAM	LVL	AGE	W	L	SV	G	GS	IP	H	HR	BB/9	K/9	K	GB%	BABIP
2016	NYA	MLB	27	6	12	0	32	32	175^2	184	27	2.7	10.6	207	46%	.340
2017	NYA	MLB	28	8	4	0	17	17	96^1	103	20	2.0	8.6	92	52%	.302
2019	MIN	MLB	30	6	7	0	19	19	100^2	113	18	3.5	7.1	80	44%	.303

Breakout: 21%   Improve: 55%   Collapse: 9%   Attrition: 5%   MLB: 88%
Comparables: James Shields, Ricky Nolasco, Dutch Leonard

When he's on the mound, there remains plenty to like about Pineda. He throws one of the hardest cutters in baseball, and because it's his primary fastball, he's pretty good at generating weak contact. The trouble is that there's no reason to believe he'll figure out how to stay on the mound. Huge and heavy and with scars all over the kinetic chain, Pineda almost made a late-season cameo in his comeback from Tommy John surgery, but had his campaign cut short by a torn meniscus in his knee. After avoiding a conversion to the bullpen for an improbably long time, he should ride the tide of the times and make the switch, even if his health limits his utility there.

YEAR	TEAM	LVL	AGE	WHIP	ERA	DRA	WARP	MPH	FB%	WHF	CSP
2016	NYA	MLB	27	1.35	4.82	3.30	4.2	96.9	51.4	15.3	44.6
2017	NYA	MLB	28	1.29	4.39	3.36	2.4	95.9	48.5	13.3	46.6
2019	MIN	MLB	30	1.54	4.92	5.38	0.0	95.7	50.1	14.5	45.6

Lewis Thorpe LHP

Born: 11/23/95 Age: 23 Bats: R Throws: L
Height: 6'1" Weight: 160 Origin: International Free Agent, 2012

YEAR	TEAM	LVL	AGE	W	L	SV	G	GS	IP	H	HR	BB/9	K/9	K	GB%	BABIP
2017	CHT	AA	21	1	0	0	1	1	6	5	2	3.0	10.5	7	19%	.214
2017	FTM	A+	21	3	4	0	16	15	77	62	3	3.6	9.8	84	39%	.304
2018	CHT	AA	22	8	4	0	22	21	108	105	13	2.5	10.9	131	38%	.327
2018	ROC	AAA	22	0	3	0	4	4	21^2	20	3	2.5	10.8	26	45%	.321
2019	MIN	MLB	23	1	1	0	22	0	23	20	3	3.6	10.3	26	37%	.293

Breakout: 12% Improve: 17% Collapse: 10% Attrition: 23% MLB: 36%
Comparables: John Gant, Jake McGee, Austin Voth

Finally healthy, Thorpe made the developmental leap for which scouts had long hoped (and for which they'd remained willing to wait, despite two-plus lost seasons). He employs a traditional four-pitch mix, but the improved consistency of his slider is especially encouraging. Any lefty who aspires to start in the majors needs a cutter or a changeup that really messes with right-handed batters, and Thorpe certainly has the latter. With enough confidence in his secondary stuff to consistently miss bats regardless of platoon matchups, he's essentially proved that he's ready for the test of big-league competition. If he passes it as impressively as he passed the Double-A test, he's a mid-rotation starter who will occasionally look even better than that.

YEAR	TEAM	LVL	AGE	WHIP	ERA	DRA	WARP	MPH	FB%	WHF	CSP
2017	CHT	AA	21	1.17	6.00	3.45	0.1				
2017	FTM	A+	21	1.21	2.69	3.59	1.5				
2018	CHT	AA	22	1.25	3.58	3.89	1.8				
2018	ROC	AAA	22	1.20	3.32	3.69	0.5				
2019	MIN	MLB	23	1.25	3.40	3.86	0.3				

LINEOUTS

Hitters

HITTER	POS	TEAM	LVL	AGE	PA	R	2B	3B	HR	RBI	BB	K	SB	CS	AVG/OBP/SLG	DRC+	WARP
Luis Arraez	2B	FTM	A+	21	258	27	14	3	1	20	19	28	2	3	.320/.373/.421	131	1.0
	2B	CHT	AA	21	195	25	6	0	2	16	13	16	2	0	.298/.345/.365	110	0.5
Randy Cesar	INF	CCH	AA	23	485	59	25	2	10	62	36	112	3	4	.296/.348/.428	115	0.8
Ryan Jeffers	C	ELZ	Rk	21	129	29	7	0	3	16	20	16	0	1	.422/.543/.578	244	1.5
	C	CDR	A	21	155	19	10	0	4	17	14	30	0	0	.288/.361/.446	144	1.2
Gabriel Maciel	CF	KNC	A	19	313	44	10	0	1	16	30	50	14	5	.287/.362/.333	102	-0.2
	CF	CDR	A	19	126	16	4	2	2	7	5	21	2	5	.263/.302/.381	102	-0.1
Jose Miranda	3B	CDR	A	20	439	52	22	1	13	72	26	51	0	1	.277/.326/.434	126	1.9
	3B	FTM	A+	20	113	9	5	0	3	10	5	11	0	2	.216/.292/.353	86	-0.3
Luke Raley	1B	TUL	AA	23	435	65	17	5	17	53	24	105	3	0	.275/.345/.477	108	0.2
	1B	CHT	AA	23	116	15	2	3	3	16	12	32	1	0	.276/.371/.449	114	0.5
Michael Reed	CF	MIS	AA	25	175	33	13	0	4	14	30	43	6	3	.314/.446/.493	177	1.0
	CF	GWN	AAA	25	229	36	13	0	7	25	32	55	4	0	.363/.459/.539	177	1.9
	CF	ATL	MLB	25	7	1	0	0	0	0	0	3	0	0	.286/.286/.286	73	0.0
Adam Rosales	INF	COH	AAA	35	428	52	22	1	18	61	38	94	3	3	.239/.313/.445	105	0.7
	INF	CLE	MLB	35	21	4	1	0	1	2	1	5	0	0	.211/.250/.421	86	0.1
Yunior Severino	2B	ELZ	Rk	18	218	32	8	0	8	28	17	52	0	1	.263/.321/.424	92	0.3
LaMonte Wade	LF	CHT	AA	24	201	30	2	1	7	27	26	20	5	2	.298/.393/.444	142	1.3
	LF	ROC	AAA	24	294	24	9	3	4	21	38	54	5	1	.229/.337/.336	98	0.5

Tremendous feel for putting the bat on the ball and for the strike zone make **Luis Arraez** an interesting prospect, but his lack of power and a serious knee injury have dimmed that star. ⓧ **Randy Cesar** broke a nice Texas League record last set in 1969 with a 42-game hitting streak, but he came well short of the nicest record in the minors, Joe Wilhoit's 69-gamer that has stood for a hundred seasons. ⓧ Beloved in every clubhouse he's occupied and formerly a fine defensive catcher, **Chris Gimenez** called it a career as a player and immediately joined the Dodgers' coaching staff. ⓧ **Wander Javier** has yet to play above rookie-ball and didn't play at all in 2018 following shoulder surgery, yet still gets plenty of prospect hype thanks to a high-upside bat and the potential to remain a plus shortstop. ⓧ Second-round 2018 draftee **Ryan Jeffers** has a great stick for a catcher, but fell that far in June because most observers worry that he won't stick behind the dish. ⓧ If there's power coming, it's coming slowly, but svelte Brazilian outfielder **Gabriel Maciel** does everything else fast, including (so far) ascend the minor-league ladder. ⓧ A versatile infielder with plenty of pop and some control of the zone, **Jose Miranda** is now tasked with proving his bat can carry a likely move to third base. ⓧ First basemen nearly always need a better approach than **Luke Raley**'s, but he can fake it in the outfield if desperately needed and there's real pop in his bat. ⓧ **Michael Reed** apparently discovered the secret to hitting while in Triple-A, which angered the baseball gods into giving him a lower back strain that ended his successful season in early September. Claimed off waivers by the Twins in November, he warrants a look as someone's fourth outfielder. ⚾ **Adam Rosales** has stuck around a remarkably long time considering he's seemingly always changing teams and never really hitting, but the secret to utility-man success is often difficult to quantify. ⚾ Where the Braves saw only a second baseman and an opportunity to exploit the international signing system, the Twins saw **Yunior Severino**, whose stick and arm will play on either side of second base. ⚾ OBP is Life, Life is OBP, and that makes **LaMonte Wade** a bon vivant worth watching, despite his dearth of other tools.

Pitchers

PITCHER	TEAM	LVL	AGE	W	L	SV	G	GS	IP	H	HR	BB/9	K/9	K	GB%	WHIP	ERA	DRA	WARP
Chase De Jong	ARK	AA	24	5	5	0	21	21	120^2	122	12	2.5	6.6	89	41%	1.29	3.80	4.91	0.6
	ROC	AAA	24	2	3	0	7	5	39^1	37	2	2.7	7.8	34	32%	1.25	3.20	4.30	0.5
	MIN	MLB	24	1	1	0	4	4	17^2	18	3	3.1	6.6	13	31%	1.36	3.57	5.23	0.0
Tyler Jay	CHT	AA	24	4	5	2	38	2	59^2	74	7	3.0	7.4	49	42%	1.58	4.22	5.67	-0.5
Devin Smeltzer	TUL	AA	22	5	5	0	23	14	83^2	94	9	2.0	7.2	67	39%	1.35	4.73	4.22	1.0
	CHT	AA	22	0	0	4	10	0	12	14	0	1.5	12.0	16	36%	1.33	3.00	2.96	0.3
Kohl Stewart	CHT	AA	23	3	4	0	14	14	68	84	3	2.8	9.4	71	58%	1.54	4.76	4.63	0.6
	ROC	AAA	23	0	3	0	7	5	40^2	45	4	2.7	6.6	30	58%	1.40	3.98	4.65	0.4
	MIN	MLB	23	2	1	0	8	4	36^2	34	1	4.4	5.9	24	56%	1.42	3.68	5.88	-0.3

Professional teammate **Matt Belisle** can still soak up innings and be wrung for goodwill in the clubhouse, so if you can find room in your organization for a good towel, you can find room for him, too. ⚾ **Alan Busenitz** typifies the late-blooming, hard-throwing, forgettable and fungible reliever: a high-90s fastball that's already flattening out on him, and a breaking ball that doesn't miss bats. And now a trip to Japan. ⚾ A spring surgery and a summer trade for Fernando Rodney have eroded **Dakota Chalmers**' already-fading pedigree, but that pedigree existed for a reason. ⚾ Pitchers long on pitchability and short on stuff, like **Chase De Jong**, can ill afford the tick down on everything that De Jong suffered in 2018. ⚾ Some other team won the World Series, but the Twins did what every other team tried to do and failed: unlock **Oliver Drake's** latent greatness, in the form of twenty strong late-season innings. Then, they cut him. ⚾ Former top-10 pick **Tyler Jay** was left off the 40-man roster and went unpicked in the Rule 5 draft, but there's still a potentially useful reliever here if his health holds up. ⚾ Southpaw and cancer survivor **Devin Smeltzer** made a midseason move to the bullpen, and to the Twins in the Brian Dozier swap. He also saw everything take off, thanks in large part to streamlining his repertoire. ⚾ With a heavy sinker and nothing else of big-league quality, **Kohl Stewart** will try to carve out a fringe career based on the name value of his pedigree as a top-five draft pick.

Twins Prospects

The State of the System:
The Twins have once again assembled a very good, very deep farm system. Perhaps it will work out better for the big club this time.

The Top Ten:

1 **Royce Lewis SS** OFP: 70   Likely: 60   ETA: 2020
Born: 06/05/99   Age: 20   Bats: R   Throws: R   Height: 6'2"   Weight: 188
Origin: Round 1, 2017 Draft (#1 overall)

The Report: Lewis was perhaps a slight surprise first overall pick in 2017, but his 2018 season made it seem silly that the Twins considered anyone else (okay, Keston Hiura should still be in this hypothetical mix, but allow me some rhetorical flourish). Lewis is a potential five-tool shortstop, and these ain't 50s and 55s. He was one of the best overall bats in the Midwest League and was 18 for almost his entire tenure in Cedar Rapids. He's got bat speed and barrel control to spare, and enough potential physical development left to project an above-average power tool to go with plus (or better) hit. Lewis will show you more loft and raw pop in batting practice as well, so he might only be a tweak or two away from finding even more thump.

He doesn't really need much more bat given his athletic tools at shortstop. We idly speculated last year that Lewis might grow off shortstop and end up in center field, but the early returns on his glove suggest he can not only stick at the 6, but be above-average there. His range, hands, and arm are all solid-or-better, and he has some room to fill out without losing his premium athleticism. Lewis is one of the best prospects in baseball now, combining projection with present performance at a premium defensive spot. What's not to like?

The Risks: Medium. Lewis doesn't have an upper minors track record yet, but the tools here are so robust, he can fall short in one or two of the five and still be a productive major-leaguer.

Bret Sayre's Fantasy Take: A power/speed middle infielder with a potential plus hit tool? That's fantasy gold right there. Lewis is likely not being talked about as a top-10 dynasty prospect yet, but there's an argument to be made that he's already there. Ultimately, I don't think he'll be elite in any fantasy category, but his all-around game could carry him toward a future as a potential top-five fantasy shortstop. Think about Lewis the way we all dreamed of Jurickson Profar.

2. Brusdar Graterol   RHP
OFP: 70   Likely: 55   ETA: Late 2020
Born: 08/26/98   Age: 20   Bats: R   Throws: R   Height: 6'1"   Weight: 180
Origin: International Free Agent, 2014

The Report: This is my least favorite blurb to write this year, because I have to admit that Craig Goldstein was right about something. All season he was in my ear about our being too low on Graterol, clashing with my general wariness about short, stocky right-handers. I like my hitting prospects to look like Jo Adell and my pitching prospects to look like… eh, to hell with it, they should look like Jo Adell too. Graterol looks like a fire hydrant. But this fire hydrant touches 101 with sink and run, and he pairs the fastball with a potential plus-plus power slider that he can front-door or run off the gloveside part of the plate with tight, late tilt. At its best, it will remind you of the Dan Warthen slider tree guys, and Graterol already has advanced command of the pitch.

Graterol's curve is a short, tight, 11-5 breaker that gives hitters a distinct look from his slider. He also tosses a very firm change in the low-90s with some sink but limited fade. The delivery is a bit stiff, and he doesn't always keep his arm speed under control, but he's generally been able to throw strikes and you don't need super-fine command at 101. Graterol is actually a bit more effective at 97-98 when he gets better movement and flashes above-average command armside. When he overthrows at the top end of his velo band, he can lose the plate or flatten out the heater. Given his size and delivery, there are reliever red flags all over the profile, but (1) he'd be a really, really good reliever with this two-pitch combo, and (2) he's shown enough present feel for spin/pitching in general that I wouldn't bet against him putting everything together with his change and command to stick in a rotation. He may look like a fireplug, but he could also look like Jose Berrios.

The Risks: High. He's a short righty who needs a more consistent third pitch and he hasn't reached the upper minors yet. Insert bullpen alarm emoji here.

Bret Sayre's Fantasy Take: There's still time before Graterol is properly appreciated in dynasty circles, which is great because once low-minors pitching prospects are, they stop being fun targets. The fireballer has the raw ingredients to be a high-upside SP2 with bushels of strikeouts, but we just need to remember that those ingredients are still pretty raw, and the Twins take a casual approach to advancing their prospects. So long as you can wait a couple more years (he probably won't realize his fantasy impact until 2022), this borderline top-50 overall dynasty prospect is worth the investment.

3. Alex Kirilloff   OF
OFP: 60   Likely: 55   ETA: 2020
Born: 11/09/97   Age: 21   Bats: L   Throws: L   Height: 6'2"   Weight: 195
Origin: Round 1, 2016 Draft (#15 overall)

The Report: Kirilloff showed no signs of rust from a 2017 season lost to Tommy John surgery. In fact, he came back looking even stronger than he did as a recent draftee in the Appy League. The bat is a rare combination of power and contact. He's a big strong kid who uses that strength well, getting leverage and barrelling up pitches. Kirilloff also shows an advanced approach, taking outside pitches to the opposite field rather than trying to pull everything. Pair that approach with an athletic frame that can handle more weight, and you can project power that will play to all fields. Defensively, he lacks the foot speed and lateral quickness for anything other than a corner position, and he may slide down the spectrum from there. Ultimately, we mostly care about the bat. It has a chance to be very good and Kirilloff should eventually find his way to the heart of Minnesota's lineup.

The Risks: High. We love the bat but, he's limited defensively, a year removed from major surgery, and yet to face advanced pitching in the upper minors.

Bret Sayre's Fantasy Take: Well, that's one way to re-introduce yourself to the fantasy community. One of my favorite bats from the 2016 draft, Kirilloff quickly worked his way back into dynasty leaguers' hearts by destroying A-ball arms and reestablishing a ceiling of 30 dingers and a respectable average. I want to see it against upper-minors arms before going all-in and declaring him a top-25 dynasty prospect, but he's on the verge and there's a good chance he'll get there by this time next year.

4

Trevor Larnach OF OFP: 60 Likely: 50 ETA: Late 2020
Born: 02/26/97 Age: 22 Bats: L Throws: R Height: 6'4" Weight: 210
Origin: Round 1, 2018 Draft (#20 overall)

The Report: Larnach isn't the easiest blurb to write this offseason (that would be Vladitio), but it's in the bottom quintile of difficulty. He's a big ol' lad who can really hit and he's going to be a right fielder... so he will need to really hit. Mashing in the Appy and Midwest League doesn't tell us much more than his 1.115 OPS as a junior at Oregon State did. Those levels were not going to be a challenge for him.

Larnach doesn't have a long track record of hitting for right-field-profile power, but again, he's a big ol' lad who hits the ball hard. He doesn't have ideal lift at present for big over-the-fence pop, but it's a pretty swing coupled with good bat speed and a strong approach. That works for Jesse Winker. Like Winker, Larnach isn't exactly going to break Statcast with spectacular plays in the outfield, but he moves well out there and has more than enough arm for right. I wouldn't expect the Florida State League to be much more of a challenge for him, and he could be one of the first college bats from his class to reach the majors.

The Risks: Medium. It's a corner profile all the way, which might limit the upside unless he can tap more into his raw power with wood bats. But he's also an extremely advanced hitter who should move quickly.

Bret Sayre's Fantasy Take: There aren't too many other bats with the combination of average and power available in dynasty drafts this offseason, making him a prime candidate for a top-five selection. Ultimately his profile isn't too dissimilar in a 5×5 roto sense from the player he has a decent chance of playing alongside in the Twins outfield soon: Eddie Rosario. Of course, if you're in an OBP league, you'll surely notice a huge difference, as Larnach could be more of a .360-.370 on-base guy in his prime.

5 Nick Gordon IF
OFP: 55   Likely: 45   ETA: Possibly 2019
Born: 10/24/95   Age: 23   Bats: L   Throws: R   Height: 6'0"   Weight: 160
Origin: Round 1, 2014 Draft (#5 overall)

The Report: The streak is over. Gordon made marginal improvements for four years running, slightly rising up the lists and staying on track for a relatively high-end outcome. He started the 2018 season along the same path, with a nice spring repeating Double-A. It was a conservative, though reasonable assignment after a successful 2017 campaign there. After his Triple-A promotion, it quickly became clear why the Twins sent him back to Chattanooga to begin with.

The competent, well-rounded Role 55 player type requires everything to stay in place. You need to keep an average-or-better hit tool; you can't hit .212 with a collapsing walk rate and no power. But that's what Gordon did at Triple-A, and it's not like the reports on him out of the International League were much better than the line above. It was an ugly summer. The defensive consensus is largely the same as it ever was—we think he has the physical ability to play shortstop, but he could really excel at second base.

Although it's a big half-grade for global rankings, we're only bumping Gordon down a half-grade for now because the broad base of skills he showed in his first four calendar years in pro ball are generally not skills you lose forever this quickly. It was a terrible three months, but it was only three months, and we're not giving up. Yet.

The Risks: Mixed. It's high variance for whether he's a good regular because he may not hit. It's low variance for a significant MLB career because there's probably enough defensive utility, speed, and name value for a utility run even if he hovers around the Mendoza Line.

Bret Sayre's Fantasy Take: Usually when we talk about prospect fatigue, we're talking about more exciting players than Gordon from a dynasty perspective. And yet here we are. Of course, when we usually talk about prospect fatigue, it's Ben or myself coaxing you through it and telling you it's all going to be okay; that your patience is about to be rewarded if you just wait a touch longer. That's not happening here. I'm out. Middle infield is not the desert it once was, and Gordon is much more blur than oasis.

6. Brent Rooker OF

OFP: 55 Likely: 45 ETA: Late 2019
Born: 11/01/94 Age: 24 Bats: R Throws: R Height: 6'3" Weight: 215
Origin: Round 1, 2017 Draft (#35 overall)

The Report: Yet another bat-first corner prospect, Rooker started horribly in 2018. This raised red flags. He was already an older prospect, reliant on the bat to carry the entire profile. I'm not one to overreact to a couple bad months—see every chat answer I gave about Francisco Mejia in April and May—but for a prospect who needs to mash, when you stop mashing, I'm gonna be a little concerned. The rest of the way Brent Rooker looked more or less like Brent Rooker (much like Mejia looked more or less like Mejia to continue this weirdo comp). That post-Memorial-Day Rooker is a passable R/R first base option, but the Mike Hessman lurking within should give you pause. The upside here is a TTO corner guy with some positional flexibility, if you include designated hitter as a position, who could bash 30 home runs and get on base enough to be an above-average regular.

The Risks: Medium. There's high profile risk, low bat risk, split the difference.

Bret Sayre's Fantasy Take: I usually like this profile more than I should, but the combination of Rooker's age and contact issues make me wary. It's Cron city, baby.

7. Akil Baddoo OF

OFP: 55 Likely: 45 ETA: 2021
Born: 08/16/98 Age: 20 Bats: L Throws: L Height: 5'11" Weight: 195
Origin: Round 2, 2016 Draft (#74 overall)

The Report: After crushing the rookie-ball leagues last year, we pegged Baddoo as one to watch in 2018, but his full-season debut was uneven at best. He's bulked up a bit and his surprising 2017 pop is less surprising in 2018. He's still a plus runner who projects well in center field. However, more advanced arms and spin gave him trouble in 2018. He's still got an intriguing power/speed combo in center—although the power is unlikely to play more than fringy in games—but his struggles against better arms are a scary harbinger for the profile. Baddoo played most of the 2018 season as a 19-year-old, so there's no need for too much panic yet, and his overall the performance wasn't even that bad. Still, the breakers don't get any easier from here on out.

The Risks: High. His adjustment to full-season pitching was rough and while he spent most of the season as a 19-year-old there are reasons to worry about the long term offensive projection.

Bret Sayre's Fantasy Take: There's more to like with Baddoo if you're in an OBP league than an AVG one, but there's potential for an OF4 future with the ability to near 20/20 in his strong seasons. Whether there's upside beyond that depends on whether he can hit .270 or not. He's likely to struggle in the Florida State League, but he'll be extremely young, and you should hang on to him if and when that happens.

Minnesota Twins 2019

8 **Jhoan Duran   RHP**   OFP: 55   Likely: 45   ETA: 2021
Born: 01/08/98   Age: 21   Bats: R   Throws: R   Height: 6'5"   Weight: 175
Origin: International Free Agent, 2014

The Report: The Twins did pretty well in their return for Eduardo Escobar, getting two prospects with an interesting collection of tools in Duran and Gabriel Maciel. Duran's fastball jumps off the scouting sheet here. It's mid-90s heat—with upper-90s in reserve—and power sink and run. It's a heavy pitch that drew swings and misses on its own in the Midwest League. Duran does spray it a bit at present, as there's a fair bit of effort in his mechanics when he wants to ramp up his arm speed, but the velocity and movement compensate for his well-below-average command of the pitch.

Duran has a power slurve that, at it's best, shows downer 11-6 break, but it's inconsistent in shape and command. The best ones show plus potential, the worst ones get spiked. There's a firm change with good tumble/split action at times as well, but it's more of a work in progress. Duran has a tall, lean, projectable frame and he should add enough bulk to start. The mechanics and stuff might not cooperate with the whole starting pitching thing, however. He's a power arm worth keeping tabs on either way, and there's impact potential as a late-inning reliever.

The Risks: High. Command and third pitch need grade jumps, no upper minors track record, might just be a late inning arm.

Bret Sayre's Fantasy Take: Welcome to the Mid-Rotation Starter Emporium. We've got secondaries with potential! We've got command issues that might get better one day! And if you spend $25 today, we'll even throw in Moderate Bullpen Risk*! Come and bring home your future SP4/5 who might be an SP3 if you ignore important pieces of the scouting report above today!

Moderate Bullpen Risk not available in Tampa Bay, San Diego or Toronto.

9 **Lewis Thorpe   LHP**   OFP: 55   Likely: 45   ETA: 2019
Born: 11/23/95   Age: 23   Bats: R   Throws: L   Height: 6'1"   Weight: 160
Origin: International Free Agent, 2012

The Report: Thorpe threw 130 innings in the upper minors after missing all of 2015 and 2016 due to Tommy John surgery and then mono. A Top 101 prospect in the Hawk Trap Guy era of prospect coverage, Thorpe's stuff has come most of the way back now and you can't quibble with the 2018 performance. I will quibble a bit with the upside in a minute here, though.

Thorpe works in the low-90s, touching 95 with some deceptive giddy-up to his mechanics and a slingy, three-quarters slot. It's a fastball-heavy approach and he commands the pitch well to both sides. It's a tricky angle for lefties and his ball has some natural cut.

Thorpe's full secondary repertoire grades out around average. There's a big slow curve that's more effective as a spot pitch than a chase offering. He mixes in a slider/cutter for a different, tighter breaking ball look and also has the requisite average change with some fade. As weird as it is to say for a dude who struck out 10 per nine in the upper minors, I'm not entirely sure what the true swing-and-miss offering is, although that hasn't been an issue so far. In the end, Thorpe checks every "Role 5 arm" box for me with a bit more uncertainty baked in because of the injuries.

The Risks: Medium. Thorpe is knocking on the door to the majors, but he might lack an out pitch and the medical history here is suboptimal.

Bret Sayre's Fantasy Take: Even being on the verge of the majors, Thorpe flirts with the fringes of dynasty relevance in leagues that roster only 200 prospects—that's not to say he shouldn't be owned in leagues of this size, but he's probably one of the first players you're looking to improve upon on your farm team. There's long-term SP4/5 upside, and AL-only relevance in the short-term, but he's unlikely to come up and take the world by storm.

10. Gilberto Celestino   OF

OFP: 55   Likely: 45   ETA: 2022
Born: 02/13/99   Age: 20   Bats: R   Throws: L   Height: 6'0"   Weight: 170
Origin: International Free Agent, 2015

The Report: Celestino is your typical teenaged toolsy center field type. He certainly looks the part in uniform, with a lean, athletic frame and a bit of physical projection left. He looks the part in the field as well. Celestino can really go get it on the grass with excellent instincts and plus closing speed. He has an above-average throwing arm as well. At the plate, he sprays line drives from a flat swing plane, although he's capable of making hard contact gap-to-gap. Celestino won't be a teenager for much longer though, and it remains to be seen how the bat will adjust to full-season ball or how much power is on the way; the teenaged toolsy center fielders sometimes end up twenty-something fourth outfielders.

The Risks: High. Yes, the speed and glove give him two major-league quality center field tools, but sometimes these dudes don't hit, and we don't know if he can hit yet.

Bret Sayre's Fantasy Take: The speed is nice, but the lack of other substantive tools and the ETA keeps Celestino as more of a name to watch unless your league rosters 250 prospects or more. If you really, really squint you could see an Ender Inciarte type here, but Inciarte himself was readily available on waiver wires in most leagues and didn't require you to hold a farm spot for three-plus years.

What the heck do we do with this guy?

??
Willians Astudillo   C
Born: 10/14/91   Age: 27   Bats: R   Throws: R   Height: 5'9"   Weight: 225
Origin: International Free Agent, 2008

In 2014, a very short, portly man showed up as Lakewood's part-time catcher and first baseman. That was and is the closest park to me, so I saw this fellow a lot. He had a hilarious skill set, like something you'd make in Road To The Show for fun. He never struck out, but never walked and never elevated the ball. He didn't look like he could throw well enough to catch, and his frame looked awkward at first. I don't know that I ever technically wrote him up, but I made a note to follow his career.

We realized during the process of this that five years later Willians Astudillo is still, somehow, eligible for this list, which means we have to deal with him. In the intervening time since that summer, he's become an even more extreme version of himself, putting up contact numbers that make no sense at all—at press time, he'd struck out just once in 189 Dominican Winter League plate appearances. But as you saw in a host of GIFs late in the season, it all just sort of works. DRC+ suggests that his underlying offensive skills are mostly real. FRAA likes his catching defense now, and he's even picked up the ability to stand at positions like second base and center field that should be physical impossibilities for him.

I have no idea what Astudillo's prospect value is in any conventional sense, so we're not ranking him per se, just sticking him down here as an interesting player to talk about. Maybe this is a plus or plus-plus hit and everything plays because of that. Maybe he hits an empty .240 in the first half of 2019 and never has a career. He's a unicorn, and that means he's probably headed down a unique career path. Enjoy it however long it lasts.

The Next Five:

11

Wander Javier   SS
Born: 12/29/98   Age: 20   Bats: R   Throws: R   Height: 6'1"   Weight: 165
Origin: International Free Agent, 2015

Jeffrey (Connecticut): Wander Javier's upside is a plus regular on the left side of the infield. This should cover all your Wander Javier questions for another year

12

Stephen Gonsalves   LHP
Born: 07/08/94   Age: 24   Bats: L   Throws: L   Height: 6'5"   Weight: 213
Origin: Round 4, 2013 Draft (#110 overall)

Gonsalves' profile was always one that would garner the "fine margins" tag. A deceptive lefty who works with a 90 mph fastball and a potential plus change, he managed to stay on the right side of those margins throughout his minor league career. His delivery has some funk and he always enticed just enough whiffs to mitigate the traffic he'd put on base. That stopped working in the majors where the margins get finer, and he walked more than he struck out in his late-season cup of coffee.

There's enough here to make a backend starter profile work. He can dial up to 93-94 when need be. His mid-80s cutter/slider thing is an effective enough gloveside weapon—particularly tough on lefties—and the change has good tumble. But the profile overall is fringy and he'll need to get more comfortable challenging major-league hitters and hope there's still enough funk and enough whiffs.

13

Luis Rijo   RHP
Born: 09/06/98   Age: 20   Bats: R   Throws: R   Height: 6'1"   Weight: 200
Origin: International Free Agent, 2015

Luis Rijo is a typical low-level Yankees pitching prospect. This checks out since he was dealt from the Yanks to the Twins at the deadline for Lance Lynn. Rijo is an athletic righty who repeats well and shows feel for four pitches. He's probably the fastest worker in baseball, a human pace-of-play initiative. The fastball sits low-90s at present but it flashes some gloveside slide and giddy-up when elevated. The curve is the best present secondary, mid-70s with tight 11-5 action. Rijo doesn't have as much upside as his fellow Luises in the Pulaski rotation—which is likely why he was the piece New York moved—but he has a backend starter projection and maybe a bit more lurking within.

14 LaMonte Wade   OF
Born: 01/01/94   Age: 25   Bats: L   Throws: L   Height: 6'1"   Weight: 189
Origin: Round 9, 2015 Draft (#260 overall)

LaMonte Wade feels like an extremely 2005 prospect crush. He's got that sexy, sexy walk rate, and he combines good knowledge of the strike zone with a short swing and plus barrel control to grind out at-bats. He's a corner outfielder, but above-average there. He could stand in center for you once a week. He has enough arm for right. He does not have enough power for either corner though. Wade "looks" like he should have more, which can almost be a harbinger of a home run spike in this day and age. He checks all the boxes for the kind of prospects we think find more power in the majors, but he's already 24… and not in the majors. He wasn't too good in Triple-A either. So for now he remains an overaged corner outfield prospect with below-average power. And in 2018, that's not #MCM material.

15 Blayne Enlow   RHP
Born: 03/21/99   Age: 20   Bats: R   Throws: R   Height: 6'3"   Weight: 170
Origin: Round 3, 2017 Draft (#76 overall)

Expectations are a funny thing. Enlow was about what you'd expect in 2018. He was 19—a third-round prep pick in 2017—taking on a full-season assignment. The results were solid across a tightly managed workload, as you'd expect. The stuff was as advertised. Low-90s fastball that was effective down in the zone, improving cutter, a curve that flashed at times.

But the concerns evaluators had about the profile post-draft played out in Enlow's first full pro season. There wasn't really a bat-misser in the profile, even in A-ball. The command wasn't as fine as you'd like considering that lack of an out pitch. The fastball was hittable up, the curve could get loopy. Nothing's really changed from last year's list. I can handwave some of the drop with "the system is improving." But it's hard to feel as excited about Enlow as I did last season, even if he still projects as the same No. 4 starter type.

Others of note:

Ryan Jeffers, C, Low-A Cedar Rapids
The Twins second-round selection makes an easy pick for this superlative in a deep system. He's a bat-first catcher who went from a small conference to the Appalachian League to the Midwest League and raked the whole way. Jeffers projects for average hit and power tools, which if he sticks behind the plate would be (thumbs up emoji). There are questions about his ability to handle the defensive rigors of catching though, and he doesn't have a traditional catcher's frame, as he's a relatively lean 6-foot-4. Also, if we were more sure he'd even be

fringy with the glove, well, he'd be up in one of the above sections. The bat might also be ready before the glove which might force the Twins hand a bit, but the bat's good enough that Jeffers is… well, worth a follow.

Ricky De La Torre, SS, Short-Season Elizabethton

De La Torre formed an intriguing double play partnership with Yunior Severino in the Appalachian League. Severino in the bigger name as one of Atlanta's free agent prospects but I think I prefer De La Torre at present. He has plus shortstop tools, can pick it, makes strong accurate throws on the run, and has good defensive instincts. He's an above-average runner and is aggressive on the bases.

De La Torre is a bit rougher at the plate. He'll muscle up and get long or try to rip it and lose control of the barrel, but when he's working with a more controlled line drive approach he covers the plate well. There's probably not enough bat in here to be a starter, but the future is very much unwritten for the 18-year-old and I like the athletic toolset at the 6, so he's one to keep an eye on.

Top Talents 25 and Under (born 4/1/93 or later):

1. Royce Lewis
2. Jose Berrios
3. Brusdar Graterol
4. Alex Kirilloff
5. Byron Buxton
6. Fernando Romero
7. Miguel Sano
8. Jorge Polanco
9. Trevor Larnach
10. Nick Gordon

Max Kepler is the only member of last year's 25-and-under list to age out, but last year's no. 1 (Byron Buxton) and no. 3 (Miguel Sano) young talents had miserable 2018 seasons that saw them demoted to the minors. That makes ranking this year's 25-and-under options tricky, which is similar to trying to figure out where the Twins stand in general right now. They still have plenty of young major-league talent, with plenty of long-term upside, but the current crop has failed to establish itself as a winning core and it's hard not to turn your attention to the next wave.

Royce Lewis is a top 10 global prospect, the gem of a vastly improved farm system, and the base around which the next title-contending Twins team could be built. That those same things were said about Buxton, and to a lesser extent Sano, just a couple years ago is a reminder that not every prospect build is structurally sound. That both Buxton and Sano still qualify for this list, and might still be potential building blocks for the Twins when Lewis arrives this year or next, is also a reminder that a wave of talent can hit the same beach more than once.

Jose Berrios is the only member of the current young core to fully live up to the hype, or at least to do so without incident. Still only 24, he's coming off his first All-Star season and is the anchor of the staff. Fernando Romero lost his "prospect" status by five innings, but he won't be 24 until later this month and ended 2018 at Triple-A. Whether you consider him a prospect or a young major-leaguer, and whether you view him as a future starter or reliever, long term he's probably still closer to Brusdar Graterol as the Twins' best non-Berrios pitching hope than many think.

Buxton is impossible to rank definitively, especially compared to Alex Kirilloff, who's yet to reach Double-A. Last year, Kirilloff topping Buxton would've seemed absurd, yet it's reasonable now and if anything Kirilloff has the stronger case to be higher. Buxton is 25. He's an amazing center fielder and runner, but he's also a .230/.285/.387 hitter who generally looks lost at the plate. Similarly, how do you compare Miguel Sano, with his various flaws now exposed, to Trevor Larnach or even Brent Rooker, for whom a positive outcome might look like… Sano?

There's still a timeline where Buxton and Sano get back on track, rejoining Berrios as building blocks, and the Lewis-led next wave turns the Twins into contenders. It's not even that difficult to picture. Lewis, Sano, Jorge Polanco, Nick Gordon, and Rooker in the infield. Buxton flanked by Kirilloff, Kepler, and Larnach in the outfield. Berrios, Graterol, and Romero atop the rotation. But there's also a timeline where this wave dissipates further, leaving only one or two long-term pieces, and Twins fans pin their new hopes on Lewis/Graterol/Kirilloff instead of Buxton/Berrios/Sano.

Part 3: Featured Articles

The Hole in The Shift is Fixing Itself

Russell Carleton

I've been on a bit of a mission against The Shift of late. I'm not out to get The Shift for the usual reasons that people oppose it. The words "the right way to play the game" won't be found on my lips. If a team wants to pursue a strategy that is within the rules and it works, then by all means, they have my blessing (not that they need it). Instead, my concern with The Shift is a worry that it doesn't work, or at least that it has a flaw that needs fixing.

The data show that while The Shift does a decent job of preventing singles on balls in play (what it's supposed to do), it also increases the number of walks that happen in front of it, and the number of additional walks outweighs the number of singles saved. It's a problem because you can't throw a guy out if he gets to walk to first base.

But the "why" was important. It seemed that The Shift was changing the way in which pitchers pitched. We saw that there were fewer fastballs thrown in front of The Shift than we might otherwise expect, and that pitchers tended to stay out of the strike zone a little more. Not by a lot. In fact, it might not even be visible to the naked eye. The percentage of pitches that are out of the zone goes from 51.0 to 53.3 from a standard defense (two right/two left) to a full shift (three on one side). That difference stands up even after we control for the types of hitters that get shifted against. And it's enough to drive up the walk rate to where it cancels out the benefits that teams thought they were getting with The Shift... and then some.

But there was some hope. I found that when individual pitchers stayed closer to the in-zone/out-of-zone mix that they used without The Shift on, they could still get the benefits of The Shift without the walk problems. So, in theory, a team could simply figure out a way to convince its pitchers to not fall prey to the walk trap and The Shift would once again be their friend.

It's reasonable to think that some teams might be more hip to this idea than others. Maybe some figured it out a year before the others. Maybe they were better at getting the message across to their pitchers. Or, maybe no one has figured it out yet.

Warning! Gory Mathematical Details Ahead!

I used data from 2015-2017, made available through MLB's data portal, Baseball Savant. They are kind enough to note when teams are using an infield shift (three fielders on one side of second base), as opposed to a "strategic shift" (someone's playing a bit out of position, but it's not quite that drastic) or a "standard" alignment.

Since we're doing this by team, I can't just look at raw walk rates, because we know that some teams have good pitchers and others have not-so-good pitchers. Some have a mix of both. I used the log-odds ratio method to take into account a batter's general walking proclivities, and a pitcher's as well, and then shoving them into a binary logistic regression. Then, I asked the computer to generate a specific coefficient for each team's pitchers, for when they went into The Shift and how that affected their walk rate.

Using those coefficients, I was able to project what would happen if a league-average pitcher faced a league-average hitter (which we expect would product a league-average walk rate; from 2015-2017, 7.7 percent of plate appearances ended in a walk) and then just switched his hat. Here's the top five and the bottom five:

Top 5 Teams	Projected Shift Walk Rate	Bottom 5 Teams	Projected Shift Walk Rate
Rockies	6.2%	Rangers	11.2%
Pirates	6.7%	Mets	10.4%
Indians	7.2%	Dodgers	10.2%
Astros	7.3%	Cardinals	9.9%
Braves	7.7%	Tigers	9.7%

There are probably people out there right now trying to figure out what the common thread is among the top and bottom teams. I'm sure, because this is Baseball Prospectus, people are already trying to make the case that sabermetric "early adopters" have some sort of edge here. I think that the more interesting piece is that by the time you get to fifth place in The Shift, we're at league average.

As a sanity check, I examined the issue on a pitch-by-pitch level, looking at how often pitchers threw their pitches in the GameDay strike zone, and again using the same basic methodology and getting team-specific coefficients. The names on the list re-arranged themselves, but the idea was the same, and the two lists correlated with an R of .593.

There's a reason that I don't usually do this type of leaderboard post. I don't really know what the Rockies, Pirates, Indians, Astros, and Braves have in common, or what they have that the bottom five don't. I can put a shrug emoji here and say, "Well, it must be something!" but that seems like a cop-out. Instead, I'd like to present another table and suggest that the table above doesn't even really matter anymore.

Year	League Percent Outside K Zone (Full Shift)	League Percent in K Zone (No Shift)	Difference
2015	54.1%	51.1%	3.0%
2016	53.3%	50.9%	2.4%
2017	52.6%	50.9%	1.7%
2018	52.0%	50.7%	1.3%

The hole in The Shift is fixing itself, and it's coming down really fast league wide. In my earlier work on The Shift, I suggested that until teams stopped having such a huge difference between their out-of-zone rate with and without The Shift on, there would just be too many walks for The Shift to make sense. It seems that all 30 of them have been working toward just that. I once estimated that it takes about 10 years for an idea to filter its way through baseball. At this rate, it looks like teams are going to catch up a lot faster than that. And yeah, they're all saber-smart now.

It's likely that whatever magic it was that the Rockies and Pirates had has made its way to Texas and Queens. Or is at least on its way. And if teams are committing to fixing the walk problem, then it's likely that they will continue shifting and shifting a lot.

And eventually it's going to actually make sense for them to do it.

—Russell Carleton is a former author of Baseball Prospectus and now an analyst for the New York Mets.

The State of the Quality Start

Rob Mains

One of the seven things you (probably) didn't know about the 2018 season is that quality starts—defined as a start lasting six or more innings with three or fewer earned runs allowed—as a percentage of total starts cratered to an all-time low of 41 percent. I want to look a little more deeply into this, since it's been a while (May of 2016, to be exact) since I've examined quality starts.

The term *quality start* is credited to *Philadelphia Inquirer* sportswriter John Lowe. It's been derided ever since he coined it in December of 1985. Three runs in six innings? That's a 4.50 ERA! In what world is that a measure of quality?

Let's start with that criticism. It's true that 3 x 9 / 6 = 4.5. (You came here for this sort of high-level math, right?) But it's also true that type of start, meeting the bare minimum for earning a quality start, is unusual. Here's the proportion of quality starts in which the pitcher lasted exactly six innings and yielded exactly three earned runs. (I'm going to confine this analysis to the 30-team era, 1998-present. Almost all data retrieved in this article is via the Baseball-Reference Play Index.)

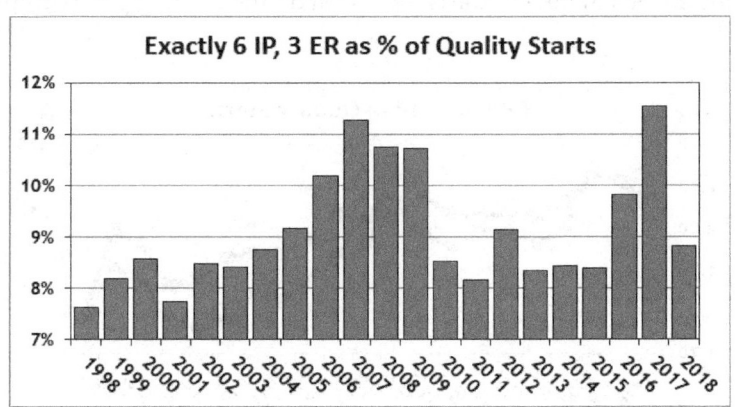

There were 1,997 quality starts in 2018. Only 176, or fewer than one in 11, featured a pitcher going six innings and allowing three earned runs. Put another way, the percentage of quality starts that resulted in a 4.50 ERA (8.8 percent) is less than half the percentage of games in which a batter hit two home runs and his team lost (22.5 percent; 237-69 won-lost). That doesn't impugn hitting two homers.

So if a 4.50 ERA isn't the norm, what is? How good are quality starts?

Pretty good, it turns out. First, on a team level:

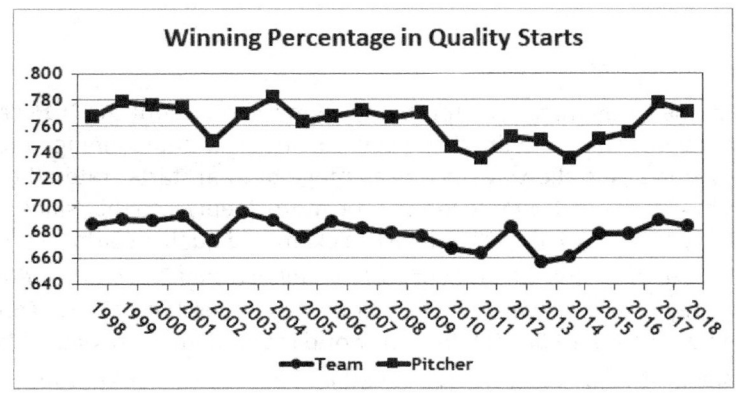

Teams receiving a quality start from their pitcher won 68.4 percent of their games in 2018, in line with the 30-team era average of 67.9 percent. A team with a .684 winning percentage wins 111 games. Getting a quality start is definitely a good thing. Individual pitchers throwing quality starts have a higher winning percentage because a big slice of team losses is assigned to a reliever.

If teams do well in quality starts, how well do the starting pitchers do? Again, very well.

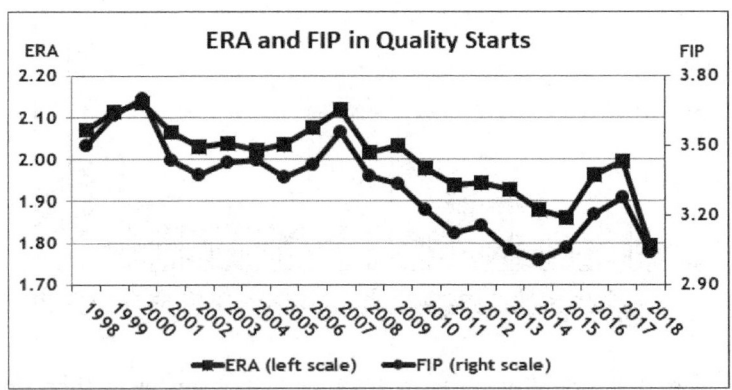

Pitchers in quality starts had a 1.79 ERA (blue line) in 2018, *the lowest in the 30-team era*. Their FIP was higher, 3.04, but still excellent. In the 30-team era, only 2014 had a lower FIP for quality starts, 3.01.

But, of course, the run environment in 2014 was different. Teams in 2014 scored 4.07 runs per game, the fewest in a non-strike year since 1976. They scored 4.45 runs per game in 2018. So surrendering a 3.04 FIP in 2018 is more impressive than 3.01 in 2014. Accordingly, let's look at ERA and FIP in quality starts relative to league averages.

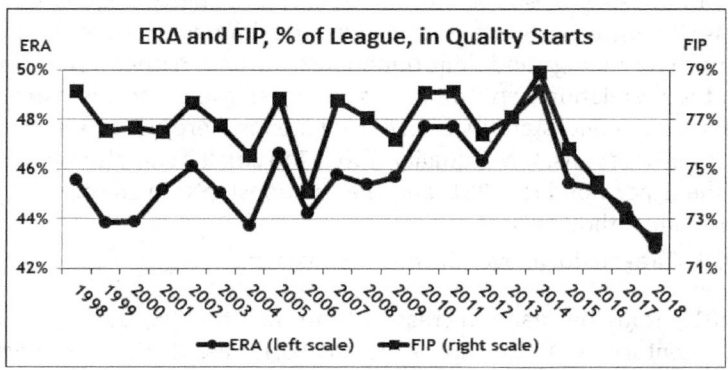

This tells a more dramatic story. Starting pitchers in 2018 gave up a 4.19 ERA and a 4.21 FIP. Starters in quality starts gave up a 1.79 ERA, 43 percent of the league average. Starters in quality starts gave up a 3.04 FIP, 72 percent of the league average. Both of these marks represent lows in the 30-team era.

The takeaway here is this: *Quality starts are better, relative to other starts, than they've ever been over the past 21 years.*

Maybe during the winter I'll look at this over a longer arc of time. For now, though, we can definitively say quality starts are the best they've ever been since the Diamondbacks and Rays joined the majors.

Yet, paradoxically, they're down.

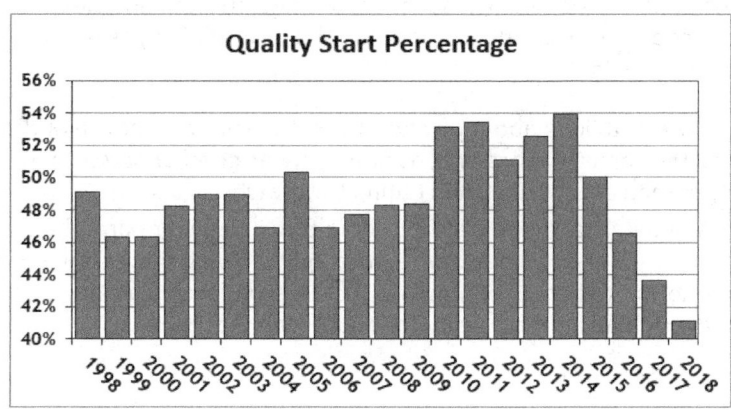

This graph covers only the 30-team era. In my article last week, though, I looked at the years 1908-2018. The result was the same. The 41 percent of starts in 2018 that were quality starts are an all-time low, well below the runners-up: 1930's 43 percent (the year teams scored an all-time record 5.55 runs per game) and last year's 44 percent.

The normal explanation for a dip in quality start percentage is an increase in scoring. When teams score a lot of runs, it's harder for starting pitchers to last six or more innings and limit opponents to three earned runs. From 1998 to 2014, the correlation between runs scored per game and the percentage of starts that were quality starts was -0.94. That means there was an extremely close relationship: More runs, fewer quality starts. Too small a sample? Go back to the start of the Expansion Era, 1961, and the relationship is even more negative, a -0.95 correlation, though 2014.

But that's broken down over the past four years:

- 2015: Runs per game increased from 4.07 to 4.25, quality start percentage decreased from 54.0 to 50.1. Yes, that's a negative relationship, but the regression model would predict a decline of 1.5 percentage points. We got 3.9 instead.
- 2016: Runs per game increased from 4.25 to 4.48, quality start percentage decreased from 50.1 to 46.6. Past experience would suggest a decline of just 1.8 percentage points. We got 3.4.
- 2017: Runs per game increased from 4.48 to 4.65, quality start percentage decreased from 46.6 to 43.6. Again, the direction's right, but the magnitude isn't. Using the relationship from 1998 to 2014, that increase in scoring should've reduced quality starts by 1.3 percentage points, not 2.9.
- 2018: Runs per game declined from 4.65 to 4.45. That should've resulted in the quality start percentage moving in the other direction, rising 1.6 points. It didn't. It fell 2.6 points, as noted, to an all-time low.

Granted, we're talking about just four years here. Maybe they're outliers. But I don't think they are. Quality starts, as noted, are as good or better than ever. But they're rarer than ever as well. And I think I know why.

To get a quality start, you need to allow three or fewer earned and pitch at least six innings. That's 18 outs. Here's a graph showing the number of starting pitchers who limited their opponents to three or fewer earned runs but got pulled after pitching at least five innings but fewer than six:

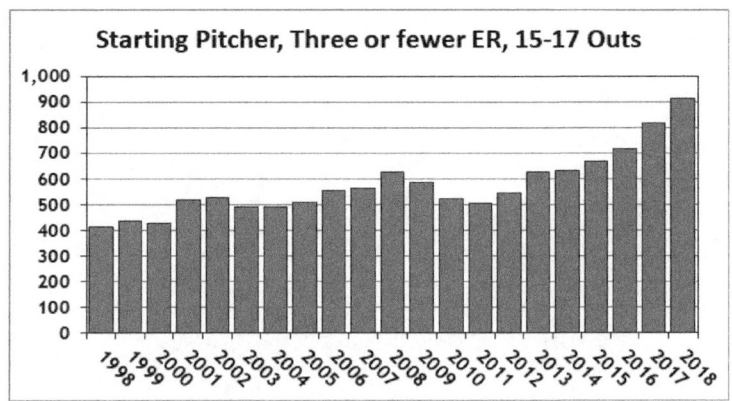

A pitcher getting 15 outs pitched five innings. A pitcher getting 16 outs pitched 5 1/3. A pitcher getting 17 outs pitched 5 2/3. More than ever before, pitchers are being removed from games in which they are within 1-3 outs of a quality start, falling just short of the six-inning finish line. Widespread acknowledgement of the times-through-the-order penalty and a flotilla of available bullpen arms is making the quality start simultaneously both more excellent and more rare.

Which is ironic, given that we saw a new post-war quality start record this season:

Rank	Pitcher	Season	Consecutive QS
1	Jacob deGrom	2018	24
2	Bob Gibson	1968	22
-	Chris Carpenter	2005	22
4	Johan Santana	2004	21
5	Luis Tiant	1968	20
-	Mike Scott	1986	20
-	Jake Arrieta	2015	20
8	Robin Roberts	1952	19
-	Tom Seaver	1973	19
-	Jack Morris	1983	19
-	Greg Maddux	1998	19
-	Josh Johnson	2010	19
-	Jon Lester	2014	19

While there have been longer streaks spread over multiple seasons, no pitcher since World War II threw more consecutive quality starts in one year than Jacob deGrom this year. The fact that he did in a year in which quality starts were the rarest they've ever been adds to the accomplishment.

—*Rob Mains is an author of Baseball Prospectus.*

Heads-Up Hacking—The First Pitch

Matthew Trueblood

Batters fell behind in a higher percentage of all plate appearances in 2018 than in any previous season for which we have pitch-by-pitch data. That kind of granular information goes back only to 1988, but we might safely assume (given all we know about baseball as it had been before that, and as it has been in the years since) that batters have *never* fallen behind at a higher rate than they did last season.

Through the 1990s, the percentage of all plate appearances that began 0-1 hovered in the high 30s and low 40s. In the 2000s, it rose steadily but slowly, through the mid-40s. In 2018, 49.8 percent of all trips to the plate began 0-1. That, as much as anything, captures in microcosm the nature of hitting in MLB today.

A countdown clock toward strike three begins ticking almost the moment a batter takes his place in the box. The league's adjusted OPS+ on the first pitch was higher in 2018 than ever before, and that has been true in most of the last 10 seasons. Batters hit .264/.289/.442 in all plate appearances in which they swung at the first pitch last season, and .241/.330/.395 in all plate appearances in which they took that first offering.

The percentage differences in batting average and isolated power there favor swinging at the first pitch by more than in any season since 1988, while the difference in on-base percentage favors taking by more than ever. If you want to get on base at a decent clip, it's a good idea to be patient, but you run the risk of missing the only chances you'll get to produce power.

Minnesota Twins 2019

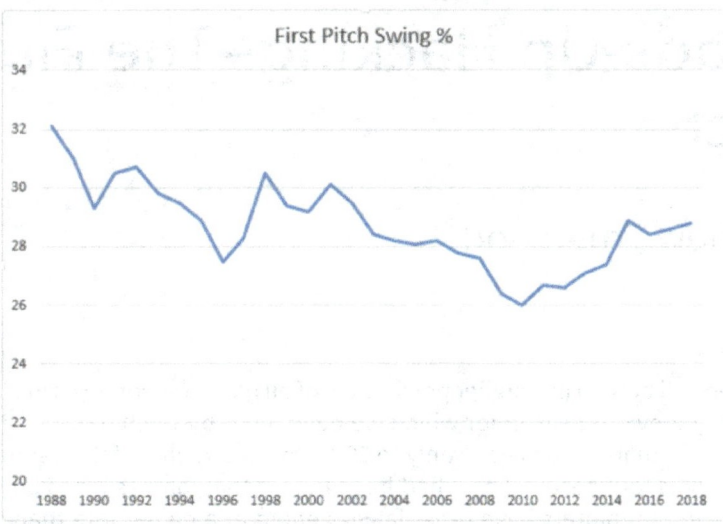

The league swung at the first pitch 28.8 percent of the time in 2018. With the isolated exception of 2015, that's the highest that number has climbed since 2002, but it might not be high enough. With the help of BP research maven Rob McQuown, I looked at the aggregate Called Strike Probability (CSProb) on the first pitch for each season since 2008, when the implementation of PITCHf/x first made measuring that possible. It's risen sharply during that period.

Called Strike Probability, First Pitch of PA (2008-2018)

Called Strike Probability is exactly what it sounds like: a pitch with a given CSProb has roughly that chance of being called a strike, if not swung at. In 2018, a batter who took 100 first pitches from a random sampling of the league's pitchers might expect to fall behind 54 or 55 times—up from 50 or 51 times in 2008. Almost regardless of pitch type (and, notably, especially in the case of fastballs), the first pitch tends to have more of the zone right now than ever before.

Pitchers are better at throwing strikes. They have better stuff, and believe more in their ability to miss bats within the zone. Perhaps most importantly, they know that batters are looking for one thing on the first pitch: a fastball. If they don't get it, they're likely to take the pitch. Check out how the use of sinkers and four-seamers on the first pitch has changed in a decade:

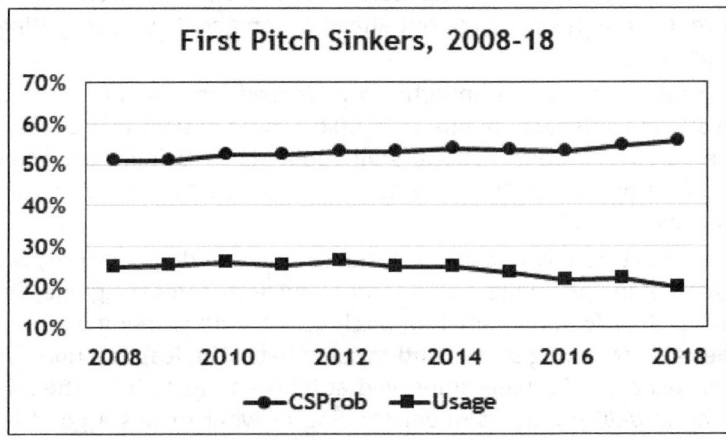

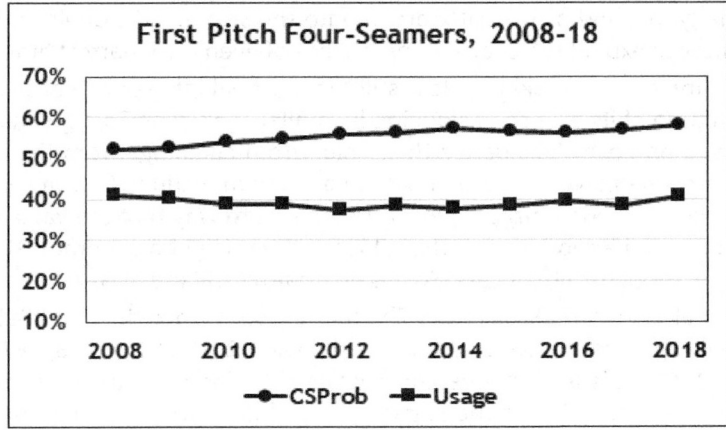

The sinker is losing its place in baseball, but the rate at which pitchers have thrown it on the first pitch hasn't dropped any faster than its usage rate in other counts. Pitchers have actually gone to their four-seamer *more* often to open counts, in the last few years, after a dip in the 2012-2015 period. What's really changed, though, and what shows up in both charts above, is that pitchers are catching more of the zone with first-pitch fastballs than they were a decade ago, or a half-decade ago. They're attacking right away, even with the pitch they know batters are expecting. The message is pretty clear: batters are being too passive.

Sliders, curves, and changeups each have more of the zone when thrown on the first pitch than they did several years ago, too, though the effect is less pronounced. Pitchers have seen the numbers; they know batters are doing better on the first pitch itself. They still feel safe throwing more and better strikes than ever before, figuring they'll come out ahead as long as they keep getting ahead to open each battle.

The Moneyball revolution brought an increased league-wide focus on OBP, which resulted in a de facto mandate to take a more patient tack at the plate. It worked very well for a while, as batters with poor plate discipline were compelled to either adjust or be expelled from the league, and pitchers with poor control were slowly weeded out.

However, concurrent with that revolution, and spurred by it in some ways, was the evolution of the pitching paradigm that now dominates the game. As batters ratcheted up their focus on inflating pitch counts and working walks, pitchers honed theirs on throwing strikes and missing bats. The league's understanding of what makes a good pitcher improved at least as much, from the mid-1990s through the mid-2000s, as its understanding of what makes a good hitter. As amphetamines and other performance-enhancing drugs were phased mostly out of the game, and as PITCHf/x broke onto the scene, individuals and teams learned how to exploit the evolved approaches of even the smartest hitters.

The ability to avoid making outs is still the most valuable one in baseball, but the magnitude of its eclipse of slugging is smaller than ever. To a greater extent than power, on-base skills derive their value from chaining—from the on-base skill levels of the players on either side of a given individual. Eleven years ago, when the housing crisis hit, people learned the hard way that the value of their homes depended a good deal on the values of their neighbors' homes. The same wasn't true, though, of their cars. So it is now, with OBP and SLG.

The global OBP in 2018 was .318. The only seasons since the Dead Ball Era in which the league got on base at a worse clip were 2013-2015, 1988, 1971-1972, and 1963-1968. This is all happening despite the aforementioned evolution of the science of hitting. It's happening despite a shift in approach and focus, one that would steer OBP ever higher, if only it were working.

Instead, it's sitting at a low ebb, and while it does so, even guys who get on base often are a little less helpful than they were 10 years ago—or 20, or 40, or 60, or 70, or 80, or 90. They're less helpful, that is, because unless there happen to be three or four other guys in the lineup who get on just as regularly, their contribution is merely to forestall the inevitable. Runs happen, increasingly, when a sudden bang happens, and that means attacking early in the count—because pitchers are sure as hell doing that.

In a league making contact on barely 75 percent of its swings, and a league in which an increasing number of pitchers can throw multiple off-speed pitches for strikes in any count, the only way to consistently generate offense is going to be aggressive. This isn't necessarily true for individuals, like Mookie Betts and Jose Ramirez, who make a lot of contact and have excellent plate discipline, and whose power comes from such natural quickness in a short stroke. Most players have to make tradeoffs, though, whether it be lowering their contact rate or raising their chase rate, in order to consistently make the quality of contact necessary to survive in today's game.

Highest %	Lowest %
Javier Baez – 48.3	Joe Mauer – 4.6
Freddie Freeman – 47.1	Mookie Betts – 9.7
Ozzie Albies – 46.3	Brett Gardner – 10.7
Jose Altuve – 44.2	Jose Ramirez – 12.0
Nick Castellanos – 44.1	Jason Kipnis – 13.8
Joey Gallo – 42.3	Jesus Aguilar – 14.5
Corey Dickerson – 40.9	Xander Bogaerts – 15.8
Salvador Perez – 40.8	Brian Dozier – 16.3
Eddie Rosario – 40.7	Mike Trout – 17.6
Nick Ahmed – 40.4	Yasmani Grandal – 17.6

Top 10 and Bottom 10 Hitters, First-Pitch Swing Rate (2018)

The question isn't which of these lists one prefers, but what they each convey, qualitatively, about the cat-and-mouse game of early-count hitting. Those top five on the left, especially, drive home the fact that for most players, getting aggressive early in the count is now key to keeping strikeout rate down and hitting for power.

For now, the message is: pitchers are coming right after batters with the nastiest stuff they've ever had. Batters had better stop giving away strike one and force hurlers to adjust, or the global OBP crisis is only going to get worse.

—*Matthew Trueblood is an author of Baseball Prospectus.*

A Hymn for the Index Stat

Patrick Dubuque

We survived without computers. I know this, because I remember the day when my dad hooked up his brand-new Atari 400 computer to the back of our 12-inch Magnavox television, and the perfect blue of the memo pad lit up for the first time. I was born just on the edge of that transitional generation, of learning cursive and balancing checkbooks and just doing math all the time, constant manual arithmetic.

It still amazes me. We learned how to sail ships without computers. We learned how to do calculus. We built towers that didn't fall down, most of the time. We engineered catapults to knock them down anyway. We built a robust system of philosophy called "utilitarianism," founded on the principle that the good of an action is evaluated by summing the effects of that action, which is the kind of formula that would make the world's mainframes crash. The whole foundation of statistics as a field is "here's math you could easily do but would die of old age first."

The fact of the matter is that there is too much math in the world to do. There are too many things changing, and too many things too small to notice, for us to handle. At some point, they become too much for the computers to handle as well, which is why we have chaos theory and undetectable earthquakes, but it's not an even fight. At some point, we fall back on intuition, and given how under-equipped we are, we're forced to bestow that intuition with some sort of supernatural superiority, the "gut feeling," that we can't prove because we can only intuit that our intuition is better.

We're all lousy at intuition, and wonderful at lying to ourselves about it. The honest truth is that computers are far better at intuition than we are, because in order to know what feels "off" you have to know what's "on." In order to do that you have to constantly reassess the average of everything, then re-rank your own experience against it.

Test your own, by comparing these three anonymous lines:

Player	G	HR	AVG	OBP	SLG
Player A	156	38	.259	.342	.535
Player B	154	38	.280	.348	.527
Player C	158	38	.266	.343	.509

These all seem like pretty similar players, right? The second one a touch more batted-ball dependent, the third a little less strong, but all pretty good hitters. And you'd be right, about the latter. Not the former.

Here's the breakdown:

- Player A: 1991 Howard Johnson, 141 DRC+
- Player B: 1996 Dean Palmer, 121 DRC+
- Player C: 2018 Giancarlo Stanton, 114 DRC+

Baseball is fortunate to have escaped the seismic shifts of so many other sports, where the talents and performances of other eras are nearly unrecognizable. (And not just other sports: try to explain the greatness of the movie Duck Soup without adjusting for era.) But they're still there, and they're nearly impossible to account for manually, without having to resort to sweeping generalizations like "steroid era" or juiced-ball era" to throw out entire swathes of production.

This is all to say that we should celebrate the index stat, that simple 100-based scale with such a humble aim: just to give context. It's hard to imagine how we lived without them for so long. Sabermetricians have always tried to make their stats look like other stats: True Average mapped to batting average, FIP molded to look like and compare to ERA. It's easy to understand the motivation—these statistics carry an emotional value in them that is hard to resist, as with the .300 hitter and the 2.00 ERA—but even they fall prey to the same loss of scale as their unadjusted counterparts. If a .300 average means different things in different years, does that hold true for a .300 True Average?

Instead, 100 doesn't say anything, except above average or below. And it does it instantly, for every season in every run environment for any statistic we want it to. We should have more index stats: K%+, so we can stop comparing Mike Clevinger's career 9.46 K/9 to Nolan Ryan's 9.55. HBP%+, so we can note that Ron Hunt was getting plunked when nobody else was getting plunked, as opposed to that imitator Brandon Guyer. Some might note how stale these references are and accuse league-adjustment as a backward-looking drive, and this is true. But we're always looking backward, always comparing the new with the expectations already set. The index stat just forces us to be honest.

There's always resistance to a new statistic, especially one so outwardly simple and so internally complex. We tend to stick with what we know, even in the case of formulas that are supposed to tell us what we know. But if your resistance is that it seems too complicated, too counterintuitive, too "black boxy," I encourage you to consider why you feel that way. Because the real world is infinitely more complicated than baseball, where all the pitches go in one basic direction and the baserunners are only allowed to travel in four directions. Baseball statistics based on mixed methodology are almost impossibly intricate. So are skyscrapers and automobiles. That's why we have computers—to take the guesswork out of them.

—*Patrick Dubuque is an author of Baseball Prospectus.*

Index of Names

Adrianza, Ehire 18
Alcala, Jorge 95
Arraez, Luis 101
Astudillo, Williams 20, 112
Austin, Tyler 22
Baddoo, Akil 86, 109
Berrios, Jose 50
Buxton, Byron 24
Castro, Jason 87
Cave, Jake 26
Celestino, Gilberto 88, 111
Cesar, Randy 101
Collins, Tim 52
Cron, C.J. 28
Cruz, Nelson 30
De Jong, Chase 102
De La Torre, Ricky 115
Duda, Lucas 32
Duffey, Tyler 54
Duran, Jhoan 96, 110
Enlow, Blayne 97, 114
Garver, Mitch 34
Gibson, Kyle 56
Gonsalves, Stephen 58, 113
Gonzalez, Marwin 36
Gordon, Nick 89, 108
Graterol, Brusdar 98, 106
Hildenberger, Trevor 60
Javier, Wander 113
Jay, Tyler 102
Jeffers, Ryan 101, 114
Kepler, Max 38
Kirilloff, Alex 90, 106
Larnach, Trevor 91, 107
Lewis, Royce 92, 105
Littell, Zack 62
Maciel, Gabriel 101
Magill, Matt 64
May, Trevor 66
Mejia, Adalberto 68
Miranda, Jose 101
Moya, Gabriel 70
Odorizzi, Jake 72
Parker, Blake 74
Perez, Martin 76
Pineda, Michael 99
Polanco, Jorge 40
Raley, Luke 101
Reed, Addison 78
Reed, Michael 101
Rijo, Luis 113
Rogers, Taylor 80
Romero, Fernando 82
Rooker, Brent 93, 109
Rortvedt, Ben 94
Rosales, Adam 101
Rosario, Eddie 42
Sano, Miguel 44
Schoop, Jonathan 46
Severino, Yunior 101
Smeltzer, Devin 102
Stewart, Kohl 102

Minnesota Twins 2019

Thorpe, Lewis 100, 110
Torreyes, Ronald 48
Vasquez, Andrew 84
Wade, LaMonte 101, 114

Ballpark diagrams for Baseball Prospectus are created by THIRTY81Project, a design concept offering original ballpark artwork, including the new 'Ballparks of 2019' 11 x 17 color print.

Visit **www.thirty81project.com** for full details.

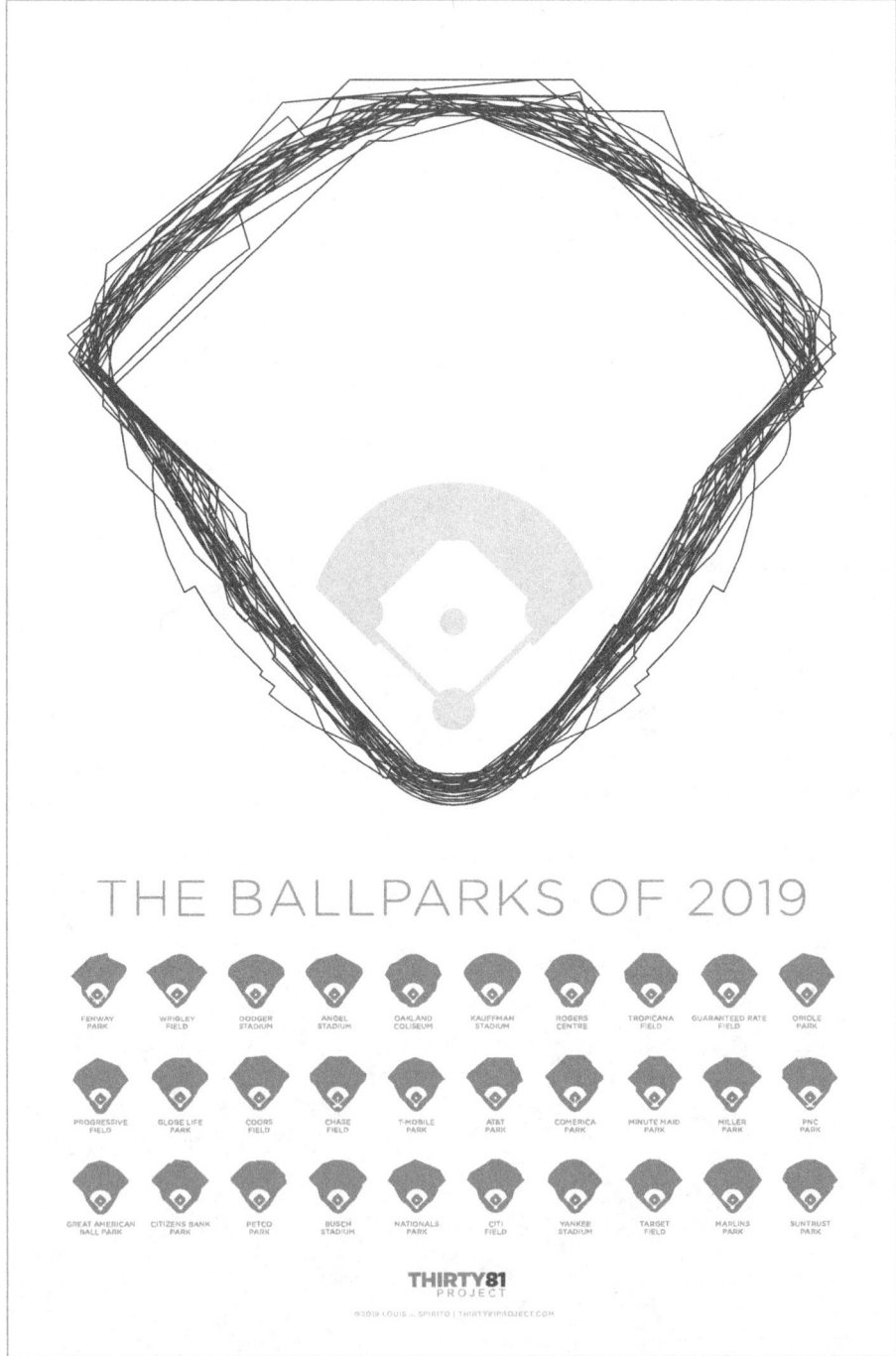